The ......

S. Vijay Kumar

JUGGERNAUT BOOKS
C-I-128, First Floor, Sangam Vihar, Near Holi Chowk,
New Delhi 110080, India

First published in hardback by Juggernaut Books 2018
Published in paperback by Juggernaut Books 2022

10 9 8 7 6 5 4 3 2 1

P-ISBN: 9789393986139
E-ISBN: 9789393986146

Typeset in Adobe Caslon Pro by R. Ajith Kumar, New Delhi

Printed at Thomson Press India Ltd

Contents

Cast of Characters

Subhash Kapoor – A celebrated art dealer based in New York. He is currently in jail in Chennai awaiting trial for the theft of idols from temples in Tamil Nadu. After his arrest, the American authorities recovered stolen Indian art worth $100 million from Subhash's warehouses and galleries, and named him 'one of the most prolific commodities smugglers in the world'.

Sushma Sareen née Kapoor – Subhash Kapoor's sister. She has been taking care of Subhash's art business and other affairs after he was arrested in 2011.

Sanjeevi Asokan – An art dealer based out of Chennai who supplied idols to Subhash Kapoor. Sanjeevi's arrest and subsequent ratting on Subhash led the authorities to him.

Deendayal – Another art dealer based out of Chennai who also supplied idols to Subhash Kapoor. The octogenarian

Deendayal was arrested in 2016. Over 200 objects were recovered from his home and warehouse in Chennai.

Shantoo – An associate Subhash Kapoor knew he could always count on. After he was arrested, Subhash asked Shantoo to try blackmailing a corrupt police officer to secure his release.

Selvaraj – A heroic police officer of the Idol Wing in Chennai and a dogged idol-thief hunter, Selvaraj managed to nab Sanjeevi Asokan and, therefore, Subhash Kapoor.

Kader Batcha – Selvaraj's deputy in the Idol Wing.

Indy – A brilliant US law enforcement officer who is investigating and maintaining a comprehensive dossier on Subhash Kapoor. The Indian authorities managed to nab Subhash before Indy could.

Jason Felch, **Michaela Boland** and **Dr Kirit Mankodi** – Associates of the author of this book, S. Vijay Kumar, who, along with him, have been helping law enforcement agencies crack down on idol theft.

Grace Paramaspry – Subhash Kapoor's ex-girlfriend and former business associate who runs an antiques shop in Singapore. Grace and Subhash had a bitter break-up which is why Grace ratted on Subhash, helping the Indian authorities get to him.

Selina Mohamed – Subhash Kapoor's girlfriend and business associate. Selina used to prepare false provenances and paperwork for idols Subhash would try to sell to museums and galleries. After he was arrested, Subhash sent a secret note asking Selina to hold on to two priceless Natarajas and two Sivakamis for him.

Aaron Freedman – Subhash Kapoor's assistant and gallery manager. He is now cooperating with the US authorities in their case against Subhash.

Prologue

Be safe, my Lord, within this earth

Somewhere in a small village near Ariyalur in Tamil Nadu: circa eleventh century CE

The artisan's deep voice reverberated around the room as he began the chant. Seated cross-legged on the floor, with both hands he held up over his head a taut loop of white holy thread. He let one end fall on his dark left shoulder, and the other passed under his right arm. Two more loops of thread lay stretched across his thighs. The chant continued as he bent to take the spoon and tip a few drops of water on his right hand and proceeded to don the rest of the threads in similar fashion.

He closed his eyes and invoked the powers of his first ancestor – Vishwakarma, the divine architect. The aroma of the kungiliyam, the sap of the sal tree, being stirred over the clay stove filled the air as he opened his eyes and gestured to his son to pour in the fine beeswax. The heat melted the golden wax, mixing it with the darker kungiliyam. He motioned for some more wax to be added

so that the ingredients were in equal proportions. He was
to fashion the main torso today.

He knew just by looking at the boiling mixture that
it had reached the desired consistency and signalled for
the pot of cold water to be brought in. The hot mixture
was strained into the water, instantly solidifying with an
audible hiss. His son looked up at him, his eyes asking if
he would like to test the result; the head-shake indicated
that it was not needed.

The auspicious hour was upon them and a large pot
of fresh water was set on the fire to boil. Several lumps
from the cooled wax mixture went into it, slowly losing
their shape. His eyes closed again as he invoked the
dyana shloka – the Vedic chant of the Lord of Dance,
Nataraja – and his hands pulled out the softening wax.
In his mind's eye he could clearly see the image he was to
fashion: the three-eyed one, Lord Shiva, twirling around,
his jatas flowing behind him, his upper arms stretched
out sideways, with a damaru or drum in one hand and
the other holding fire. The left leg went up and then the
two lower hands formed their mudras – the left hand
forming the gaja, that mimics the trunk of an elephant,
with the fingers pointing gracefully downwards towards
the raised foot, signifying the Lord's capacity to remove
obstacles and hindrances; and the right hand displaying
the abhaya, where the fingers point upwards and the
palm is facing the viewer, symbolic of the Lord telling the
devotee not to fear because he is there to protect him. He
smiled as he envisioned the brilliant aureole that encloses
the entire composition burst into flames. A dazzling light

seemed to emerge from the Lord's nabhi, or navel, slowly growing in luminosity, permeating the entire room with its radiance. His ears picked up the sound of his Lord's anklets jingling in perfect rhythm with the beat of the primordial drum as his fingers worked to fashion the wax.

His eyes became moist with emotion as he stood back to review his work, before realizing that he had merely repeated what had been handed down to him through the ages – a thousand years of knowledge flowed through his hands, the accumulated wisdom of his ancient, unbroken bloodline coursed through his veins. This would be his best creation and he would make it unique with his signature embellishments. But for that he needed a different consistency of the mixture. He gestured to his son to add more wax to make it one and a half parts of wax to one part kungiliyam.

Outside, the donor waited anxiously. He had commissioned the bronze sculpture and paid for the metal, but today was extra special. His wife had good news for him – she was pregnant, and she assured him that it would be a boy. He had brought four of her heaviest gold chains as an offering. They would be melted and go on to make his resplendent Lord glitter and, in turn, make his progeny's fate glitter as well.

But first, the artisan had to make a clay cast of the wax Nataraja into which would be poured the molten metal.

Ten days later, at the appointed hour, they assembled in front of the garbhagriha or the sanctum sanctorum, and he placed his masterpiece on a raised platform. As the lamps were brought in closer, the play of light and shade seemed to bring the statue to life, the Lord of Dance, Natesa.

Sometime in 1311 CE

It was not yet light, but that the village was already up was evident from the unusual and frantic sounds at that early hour. Urgency spread through the priest's hands as he grappled with the thick coir rope, knotting it over the neck of a brass pot. He gave a final tug to the ends to ensure the knots were tight and sent it over, into the temple well, and waited for it to hit the water. His hands alternated as he pulled the pot up, the well-oiled mechanism of the wooden pulley hardly making any sound. He uttered the Lord's name as he poured the water on his head, his long tresses falling over his eyes. He brushed them aside and dropped the pot into the well once again. The cold water helped calm his nerves. He repeated this ten times and then emptied the pot into a larger brass drum. He bent low into the drum to use the water to rinse its sides clean and poured out the contents. The pulley was worked another ten times before the drum was full and he turned his attention to the smaller silver pot next to it. He meticulously cleaned it too, before filling it up. His hair had dried by the time he was done, though his dhoti, still wet, clung to him. He twisted his locks into a knot behind his head.

He picked up the brass drum and the silver pot. Filled with water, they were heavy, but his heart was heavier.

He had consulted all his charts the previous night.

The news of the evening correlated with the stars. Saka year 1232 (1311 CE) was not easy to read. He tried to see his future but a dark cloud shrouded it. He tried to read the chart for his son, but it just refused to speak to him.

He had made his decision then. He knew that the day had finally arrived. It was the day of supreme sacrifice. His grandfather had told him about it when he was very young, and his father after that, several times, so that he would know exactly what to do. Every step had been clearly laid out. It was all preordained.

He had the large key to the temple's main door tied in a thick red thread around his waist. There were a few smaller locks to open as well, and an iron crossbar to remove, so he left the vessels near the door and pushed the long-necked ancient key into the thick wooden wicket door – the small door within the door. He stooped low as he passed through the small opening and reached for the massive crossbar that barricaded the main door of the temple. There was a single lamp still burning at the side of the garbhagriha. He walked towards the lamp, added another wick to it and topped up the oil from the container by the side. He opened the door of the garbhagriha and lit a few more lamps before going back to fetch the vessels. Usually he would head straight inside to the main deity, but today was different. He would break tradition.

In the fifteen-odd years he had been the head priest and the fifteen years he had been his father's apprentice before he passed away, and for generations before him, it had never been done. He turned to where the utsava murthis, or processional idols, were stored. In south

India, the main deity is fixed in one place inside the sanctum sanctorum and cannot be moved. The deity, usually made of stone, is called the moola murthi, moola bera, or moolavar. Moola literally translates to main or principal. In Shiva temples the moola murthi is generally a linga. During festivals and on special occasions, the various avatars of Shiva or Vishnu are displayed before the public in the form of bronze idols which are taken out in a procession. These are the utsava murthis and on specific days specific avatars of the gods are brought out on wooden vahanas or vehicles. Even when not in procession these utsava murthis are treated as living beings. They are taken at night to their sleeping room called palli arai (palli means sleep and arai room) to the accompaniment of ritual music and lullabies. In the morning, they are woken up lovingly with similar songs, bathed, attired in fresh clothes and fed before being placed in front of the moolavar.

As the priest opened the small grille door, he started singing to his gods – a waking-up hymn. He brought in the silver pot and slowly poured water from it over his dancing Lord, the Nataraja, his consort Sivakami (Parvati is called Sivakami when she is witnessing the dance of Shiva), then on the divine family – Shiva, Uma (another name for Parvati) and Skanda – as Somaskanda, then the ever-present form of Appar with his signature tool to clean temples – the uzhavaram, and lastly the large Ganesha. He took out the pulp of the tamarind he had brought with him and used it to scrub the idols before washing them again. He continued to sing to his gods even as his hands worked. Then he untied the cloth around his waist and dried them individually, taking care to wipe under their arms, in the back and in the niches between the locks of the Nataraja. His hands felt the cheeks of his Lord as he wiped the drops of water that had fallen on his neck and chest.

He did not realize how long he had been there until he heard his men assemble near the main door of the temple. They could not be here so early! His young son was also with them and he came into the temple bleary-eyed, half-awake due to being woken up so early.

The men were tense and it showed in the way they carried their tools. There were eight of them and they carried an array of crowbars and spades. The boy ran up to his father and held his hand. He wiped the moisture off the idols one more time and stood straight to offer his prayers. He turned and walked outside with firm steps. The men followed in silence now.

He walked along the tall outer wall of the temple, all the while counting his steps and looking at the sculptures carved on the pillars, till he came to one which showed a lady dwarf blowing into a conch. He stopped and took three steps to his left. He was standing on top of a heavy granite slab which appeared to be no different from the rest that were laid to form a pathway around the temple. He motioned to his son to come near and whispered something in his ear before calling the men. They used a small crowbar to prize out the stone block. Surprisingly, after only a few nudges it came loose. They slipped a stout rope under it and pulled to slide it to the side. Only then did they notice that the slab was only half the thickness of the adjoining ones.

Immediately, they took their spades and started digging out the soil underneath. Very soon, four of them were up to their waists in the pit. They looked up to check if they should stop, but he shook his head and indicated they should dig up to their necks. The pit had to be over five feet deep.

When they had finished, they placed a large granite slab at the base of the pit and spread kusa grass evenly over it. He had prepared the granite slab and the kusa grass the evening before, just as his manual had stated. He sprinkled water on the grass and invoked the protection of Mother Earth. Finally, the idols were carried, reverentially, one by one, and placed carefully over the grass.

Far away in the distance, dark smoke rose and the air was filled with the odours of death.

They took turns to put earth into the pit and then replaced the stone to cover it. By the time the excess earth and sand were dumped into the well, there were no telltale marks of their morning's labour.

The air had grown thicker as the shouts became shrieks. The men held their crowbars and spades and positioned themselves outside, against the temple's main door.

The sound of galloping horses made him run to the garbhagriha. He prayed for the final time, not for himself but for his son to survive, not out of love but so that he would be able to find the spot and restore his Lord to his rightful abode. The invading armies of Alauddin Khilji, led by Malik Kafur, had taken temples ten times the

size of his in no time. They were here. The twang of the
enemy's bows and the whizzing of arrows accompanied
the cavalry's frenzied cheers outside as the archers killed
the assembled men within minutes, and opened the
temple's doors. They did not waste time breaking anything
that was not of value. They tested their metal weapons
on the stone sculptures. He pleaded with them to spare
the gods, but to no avail.

They dragged him by his hair into the street, to the
commander who was dressed in full armour. The entire
village had been laid to waste already. Next to him was
the village elder, his face a bloody mess. They asked
him where the gold was, by showing him a bag of gold
ornaments – loot from the previous day's plunder. They
cut off the elder's ears and then his nose, yet he did not
speak. So they took out his tongue and threw it to the
dogs. Then they turned to the priest.

They wanted gold or any metal idols that they could
melt. They dragged him back into the temple and took
turns to slam his head against the stone pillars. They
bound his legs and tied him to a horse and dragged him
out onto the street where he saw his young son's body,
struck with countless arrows, lying face up. In his dying
breath he managed a final prayer.

'Be safe, my Lord, within this earth as long as it
pleases you.'

A few seconds later his body lay on the ground as his
soul merged with his Creator.

Did this really happen? I'm not sure. But it is how I imagine the histories of our idols. How they were made with deep devotion; how several were destroyed; and how a number of our gods came to be buried deep inside the earth. For more on the burying of gods when there is a threat to them, see Appendix 1.

1

The Glamorous Life of
Subhash Kapoor

March 2007

'$8.5 million for the pair!'

That's what Subhash Kapoor, a prominent art dealer who ran a gallery called Art of the Past in New York, was selling two incomparable Chola-era idols of Nataraja and Sivakami for – the kind temple priests would readily give up their lives to protect.

From 850 CE to 1250 CE the Chola dynasty witnessed the building of many elaborately carved stone temples all over Tamil Nadu, which, as mentioned in the Prologue, housed the main deity made of stone along with a number of processional bronze idols adorned with sumptuous silks and dazzling jewels. These fine Chola bronzes are highly coveted by museums and collectors. They are the star attractions of the India collections in many art institutions around the world. What Subhash

Kapoor was selling in March 2007 for $8.5 million was a 3.5- foot-tall and approximately 150 kg Nataraja – Lord Shiva performing the bewitching dance of creation and destruction, surrounded by an enormous circle of flames and his much shorter and lighter consort, also surrounded by a stunning oval of flames, the beautiful Sivakami. The pair dates back to the twelfth century CE.

Subhash frequently conducted sales meetings in one of the fancy steakhouses on Madison Avenue in New York. It wouldn't be surprising if a buyer responded with bewilderment at the price Subhash Kapoor was quoting. Such prices were unheard of even for the best of Indian art. But then this was no ordinary sales pitch for an ordinary piece of art. This pair was incomparable, the likes of which had never come up for sale in the art world. At this point the pair was still in India, and Subhash had a photograph of the idols with him.

In recorded public history, there has only been one other instance of a matched Nataraja bronze with his consort Sivakami outside India and even in that case the Nataraja was gifted to the Metropolitan Museum of Art (MET), New York, by Robert Ellsworth in 1987, but he sold off the Sivakami to a private collector in 1990 and it disappeared from public view for a long time after that.[1] The Ellsworth Sivakami was later offered for sale again in 2013 by Sotheby's auction house and it went for $137,000.[2] But Kapoor's matched pair was far superior to Ellsworth's and was expected to fetch a hell of a lot more.

For one, the Nataraja and Sivakami that Kapoor was trying to sell had a rare inscription on their pedestals and it is extremely unusual to find inscribed Chola bronzes. That increased their importance since it showed unambiguously that they were a matched pair – that is, they were from the same temple. The inscription read 'Suthamalli' in the Tamil script, which is the name of the village they are from. But there was a problem. Yes, the Suthamalli bronzes were in a league of their own but the pair had never been exhibited, studied, or included in art books or catalogues before. Where had

Institut Français de Pondichéry / École française d'Extrême-Orient

Suthamalli Sivakami

Suthamalli Nataraja

they suddenly appeared in New York from? This could be a pressing question for a buyer because, according to an Indian law passed in 1972, any antiquity older than 100 years cannot be taken out of the country. If such an antiquity is discovered to have been taken out of India after 1972, then, under the terms of a UN convention, the recipient country has to forfeit it without compensation. This would have been a stumbling block for a museum interested in buying the pair from Kapoor. But the art dealer had his distinct ways of sweetening deals to overcome such speed bumps. A lavish private viewing for a museum acquisitions committee and its major patrons, authentication by a prominent academic art historian, and a few free paintings and artefacts as well would not be unheard of for a sale of this value.

Indeed, Kapoor knew how to close deals. Just recently, the Asian Civilisations Museum (ACM) in Singapore had booked a spectacular Chola Uma, another name for Goddess Parvati, that he was selling. And in what should give you an idea of how significant an art dealer Kapoor was and the rarity of the works he offered for sale, he had another Chola era Nataraja, from the same temple in the village of Sripuranthan in Tamil Nadu. Subhash managed to pull of several art world coups in terms of the exquisite pieces he offered for sale. He hadn't been able to find a buyer for the Sripuranthan Nataraja yet, though. And so if the Suthamalli pair – at $8.5 million – was too expensive he could offer a buyer the Sripuranthan Nataraja instead. The price tag? Just $5.1 million. That Nataraja would later be scooped up by the National Gallery of Australia (NGA) in Canberra.

Born in 1949, Subhash had an older brother, Ramesh, and a younger sister, Sushma. Their family had moved from Lahore to Jalandhar prior to Partition when his father realized there was a business opportunity in dealing in rare books and manuscripts left behind by families fleeing the horrors of the divide. By 1962, the family had moved to Delhi where Kapoor's father started a gallery that specialized in Pahari paintings. Kapoor studied at

Subhash Kapoor

DAV School in Delhi and along with Ramesh he helped with the family business. In 1974 Kapoor left for the US where he continued in the same line of work, and in 1976 he married his wife, Neeru. Ramesh and Sushma also moved to the US by 1976, and by 1981, they had all become US citizens.

That a child, whose father was a small-time art dealer, had become one of the most prominent figures of the international art circuit was no small achievement.

Kapoor's gallery, Art of the Past, was located on the corner of Madison Avenue and 89th Street, in the moneyed Upper East Side of Manhattan and very close to the MET, the Guggenheim and the Cooper-Hewitt – the top art institutions of our time. He was no stranger to the world of oysters, rare beef steaks and even rarer wines. Slightly round around the middle, and balding, he dressed impeccably in fine suits and silk ties and wore rimless spectacles. He was well heeled enough to effortlessly fit into the champagne-and-caviar world of Manhattan art parties and museum galas, as well as at blue-blood auction houses and in haughty academic circles.

Take a walk in the Smithsonian and you're likely to encounter Subhash Kapoor's name on a plaque more than once. He had worked hard to edge his way into the museum circuit, often gifting extremely valuable works of art, such as the Shunga period (200 BCE–50 CE) pot that he gave to the MET in the name of his daughter.[3] The exponential increase in one's brand value and public profile by having a plaque next to the opening exhibit of the MET's India collection that says 'Gift of Subhash Kapoor, in honour of his daughter, Mamta Kapoor, 2003' cannot be underestimated. It greases the path to being viewed sympathetically by museum acquisitions

The Metropolitan Museum of Art, New York

Subhash Kapoor's gift to the MET in honour of his daughter

committees in the future. When his father died in 2007, Kapoor again gifted the MET a group of artworks in memory his father from whom he had learned his trade. And who, according to the *Indian Express*,[4] had been tried for art theft in the 1970s. He also loaned artefacts to hotels such as The Pierre, New York, where the super wealthy were sure to encounter them and his name on a plaque next to them.

So how had Subhash Kapoor risen to such impressive heights? Till 1994, Subhash had been a small-time gallery owner in New York. At some point he had started selling terracotta artefacts from Chandraketugarh – a much vandalized 2500-year-old site in West Bengal, India, that had been continuously occupied from the pre-Mauryan era (around 600 BCE) through to the Pala–Sena era in the twelfth century CE. The site was originally excavated by Calcutta University in the mid-1950s but then it was effectively abandoned in the mid-1960s. In the 1950s there was already a law in place 'forbidding export of archaeological material. So any material from the region up for sale has been illegally excavated and exported.'[5]

These artefacts filled Subhash's coffers for several years, thanks to the steady market for the small, delicate terracottas. Subhash was able to sell and even donate hundreds of them to collectors and museums. The Shunga era pot that Subhash gifted to the MET, for instance, is from Chandraketugarh.

Around 1994, Subhash was able to take a small step forward in his business. He managed to sell to the prestigious Art Gallery of New South Wales (AGNSW) two terracotta artefacts from Chandraketugarh. The AGNSW finalized the acquisition of the two terracottas with scant paperwork or provenance and transferred the agreed sum of $14,500 to his company, Art of the Past. The items entered the AGNSW collection as terracotta numbers 1376 and 2131.

This was the start of a long association with the AGNSW. Subhash ensured his gallery assistants sent regular portfolios to the museum, predominantly dealing with paintings. He had regular sales with them, including two paintings in 1995 for $62,500, a Kerala dance mask in June 1998 for $7,500 and a Mewar school miniature painting of Shiva for $3,500.

But Subhash still needed the big break, the big-ticket sculpture sale that would catapult him into the top league. And for that he had to wait for help from the man with the golden touch.

This person was a frequent visitor to his gallery and someone who had helped in a big way to bring Indian art to American shores, not as an art scholar like Ananda Coomaraswamy, but as a catalyst for collectors, virtually putting a price tag on every Indian art item – Chola bronzes, Gupta stones and so on. He had billionaires and Hollywood celebrities eating out of his hand, buying stuff for their personal collections and donating a part to the museums which he recommended. An associate of a major art magazine, he was a leading historian and a celebrated scholar. One of his books on Indian art has generous references to items that have passed through Subhash's hands.

Subhash Kapoor had invested heavily to get this scholar to recommend him to the big names in Australia. The Art of the Past advertisements in the magazine associated with the scholar were a masterstroke. Through the advertisements Subhash could curry favour with the scholar while at the same time consolidating his brand and creating legitimacy for his items and his business. Magazine advertisements create very useful points of reference for museum acquisitions committees.

Finally, around 1995, he got the scholar's valuable recommendation. The scholar advised him to lend, and the AGNSW to accept, some pieces from his collection for a mega exhibition at the museum. Subhash jumped at the opportunity. Soon, six objects and three paintings landed in Sydney for Dancing to the Flute: Music and Dance in Indian Art exhibition in June 1997.

The organizers sent a personal invite for Subhash and his brother Ramesh to attend the exhibition, and even booked them under the corporate rate of the AGNSW at Hotel InterContinental, Sydney. (Ramesh runs his own Kapoor Galleries in New York and claims he has no connection to his brother any more.)

Subhash learnt a lot during that visit and fine-tuned his modus operandi – and it paid off. Even though he had already sold many items to the AGNSW, the sale of a Pala dynasty Varaha sculpture to them in 1999 was a significant event. One, it marked a shift from selling paintings and small terracottas to dealing in sculptures, where the megabucks are. And, two, it marked the flowering of his relationship with the scholar who was instrumental in setting this up and also assisted in the negotiations. And so, after much deliberation the deal was finalized at $12,000. Don't be fooled by the relatively low price point. The significance of the deal lay in the induction of Subhash Kapoor into the world of museum sculpture and raising his prestige.

Soon enough, Kapoor was striking deals worth hundreds of thousands of dollars with his Australian clients. In 2004, he sold to the AGNSW an Ardhanarishvara idol, depicting the androgynous form of Lord Shiva and Parvati, for $300,000. And then the following year he sold a Sharabanimurthi (a fierce form of Durga where the goddess has the body of a woman but the face of a lion; also identified as Pratyangira or Narasimhi) to the NGA for AUS$328,244.

Subhash had raked in half a million US dollars on just those two sales. He was making waves in the big league. And then there was no looking back.

In 2011, Subhash Kapoor was arrested by Interpol in Germany for art theft, particularly that of idols from two temples in villages in Tamil Nadu whose names you've already heard: Suthamalli and Sripuranthan. Kapoor was subsequently extradited to India where he awaits trial. His arrest caused an earthquake in the art world, the tremors of which are still being felt. Stolen art that can be traced to him is being discovered on every continent, in important museums and collections. And his associates are being rounded up and arrested one by one. This is the story of how Subhash Kapoor was caught. But don't think of him as just a harmless art thief like those charming villains in old black-and-white movies. In 2012, when the US authorities raided Subhash's warehouses in New York they recovered stolen art worth $100 million. This was just the inventory he had been maintaining. The man had been in business for over three decades by that time. Think of the actual scale of his empire. No wonder the US authorities called him 'one of the most prolific commodities smugglers in the world'.[6] This was serious crime, not fluff.

But what do I, a lay shipping executive from Singapore, have to do with this story? I may be a shipping executive by day but I like to think of myself as an art-thief-hunter by night. Around 2007–08 I started a blog on Indian art called poetryinstone.in. That blog unwittingly got me involved in the capture of Subhash Kapoor. Since then I have been in deep contact with both the Indian and the American authorities, trying to do my duty and help nab the bad guys and bring our gods home. I'm just trying to do my small bit, that's all. In the process I've learned a lot about art and the rotten art world and have started giving lectures and participating in seminars and suchlike on Indian art – which the academic community and the commercial art world both hate.

Before we go on I must introduce you to Sanjeevi Asokan, one of Subhash Kapoor's main idol suppliers. Let's start at the beginning: the looting of the temples of Suthamalli and Sripuranthan.

2

The Suthamalli and Sripuranthan Heists

When I took on the task of studying and exposing the rampant looting of our cultural treasures and our gods, it did occur to me to review the risks. This would come up after every Q&A session with the media or during interactions after talks that I gave. The personal risk I was exposing myself to was high. I have had unannounced thugs turn up at my lectures in Chennai. Organizers were told not to invite me to participate in prestigious seminars. I have been critical of the law enforcement machinery, the hypocritical art world, and the crooks alike, and so I've made enemies everywhere. I have had threatening emails asking me not to cooperate with the US law enforcement agencies. And of course, the biggest threat: even after they're arrested suspected thieves are let out on bail routinely. But I was inspired to push on by something I chanced upon in the book *Early Chola Temples* by S.R. Balasubrahmanyam.

> Four persons are said to have made a false claim to
> certain *devadana* lands [Land that has been donated
> to God]. To prove the title of the lands [belonged]
> to the temple certain members of the Tiruchchula
> Velaikkarar sacrificed their lives by plunging into fire
> . . . the Tiruchchula Velaikkarar were Saivite devotees
> to safeguard the interests of temples and their properties
> even at the sacrifice of their lives.[1]

Here were custodians who were prepared to sacrifice
anything to protect the property of Shiva! Often, the
role of the custodians goes uncelebrated. Many of them
do not do this as a job, or for wages, rewards or awards.
They consider it their duty.

One such custodian was Kalyaniammal of Suthamalli.

The once famed Sri Varadaraja Perumal temple
(devoted to Lord Vishnu) of Suthamalli had been lying
in ruins for a few decades and was a pale shadow of
its tenth-century glory. Kalyaniammal's rundown hut,
located between the main road and the dilapidated gates
of the ancient temple, was in no better shape. She lived
alone. She had the keys to the temple and wouldn't let
anyone in except, on rare occasions, usually festivals, when
a priest came from the nearby town to do the puja.

The villagers called her a mad woman but knew well
enough not to mess with her. (During the course of my
pursuits I have come across many such 'mad' women
with keys to dilapidated temples, but never had trouble
dealing with any of them!) Her once large family had
been the traditional custodians of the temple and lived

on a monthly allowance from the village council. How she managed to eke out her living when the practice was discontinued was a mystery. She was the one last vestige of the past and then she, too, was gone in early 2000, leaving the temple's protection to a rumoured swarm of killer bees and a rusty old grille door. Why she went or where she went, no one knows.

The village had a Shiva temple as well, the Sundareshwarar temple, which was in much worse condition, having been unopened for years. In early 2000, officials of the Hindu Religious and Charitable Endowments Board (HR&CEB) turned up at Suthamalli village and decided to move the bronzes from the Sundareshwarar temple to the Varadaraja Perumal temple in order to keep them safe. At least the Varadaraja Perumal temple was opened every three–four months. Interestingly, the HR&CEB never documented the idols by photographing them – an error that would cost them dearly in the future.

Tamil Nadu has more than 50,000 temples under the management of the HR&CEB, which did away with the millennium-old tradition of hereditary trusteeships and is mired in a host of scams related to mismanagement of temple funds, non-collection of dues from temple lands, improper and fraudulent renovations and theft of assets. The sad fact is that even though many people believe that public funds should not be devoted to 'rich' temples, only a handful of 'famous' temples, not even 10 per cent of these 50,000 temples, have annual revenues over ₹10,000 or $150.

From 1925, when the first version of the HR&CE Act was promulgated, it has gone through many iterations. Under the current law in Tamil Nadu, the management and control of temples and the administration of their endowments is one of the primary responsibilities of the state.

If the HR&CEB was one of the adversaries that Subhash Kapoor and Sanjeevi Asokan had to contend with, the other was the Idol Wing. You will soon see why they were relatively easy challengers for Subhash and Sanjeevi to deal with.

The Idol Wing is a special law enforcement unit in Tamil Nadu dealing specifically with cases of idol theft worth over ₹5 lakh. Set up in 1980, it met with great success in reducing the number of temple robberies at first. Why? The reduction was the direct result of a series of phased moves undertaken by the Idol Wing, the most significant being the elaborate and time-consuming task of shifting the more valuable idols from remote temples in the countryside to larger temples in the more populated areas.

In 1984, V. Ramakrishnan, head of the Idol Wing, said, 'To date, we have removed nearly 3,000 Chola icons from unprotected temples to larger temples and museums.' But 3,000 antique idols of less value still awaited removal at that time and the programme is still going on in 2018.[2]

Some progress has been made over the years. Several central icon centres have been built to house idols. Temple authorities can borrow their idols during festivals but they have to give them back once the rituals and celebrations are over. However, these centres are only for bronze idols – stone sculptures still remain unguarded in temples.

Unfortunately, it can take months, sometimes even years, for temple thefts to be discovered, and in many cases, the authorities have no record of what all the temples housed. In that sense Subhash and Sanjeevi had chanced upon the perfect crime. A crime that often goes undetected for years. A crime where no one is quite sure what was stolen in the first place.

Both the Idol Wing and the HR&CEB have failed miserably at their job so far. Despite being in existence for many years, they still haven't built an asset archive for the temples. How can any progress be made in the absence of such basic measures?

According to police records, in May 2005, an innocuous-looking Subhash Kapoor checked into the posh Taj Connemara, one of the oldest art deco hotels in Chennai. He could have passed off as any other Indian businessman who stayed at the hotel and the receptionist didn't bother to ask for his passport or identity card – a mandatory requirement now – but not back in 2005. A few hours later, Sanjeevi Asokan joined him. This is thought to be the first time they met. To the outside world Sanjeevi seemed a respectable art dealer. Originally from Kerala, he moved to Tamil Nadu several years ago. He lived in the Triplicane neighbourhood of Chennai and had an art gallery at Parry's Corner, aside from several other offices/galleries in Tamil Nadu and Kerala. Little did anyone know at that time that Sanjeevi and Subhash were together plotting the biggest heist of Chola bronzes in history.

This is what happened according to the official report of the Idol Wing:[3]

Sanjeevi knew the 'topography' of the ancient temples of Tamil Nadu like the back of his hand. He also had a well-developed network of 'idol offenders', foot-soldier thieves who would willingly do the actual looting for a fee, a relatively low fee compared to the prices of the idols they were stealing. Sanjeevi would refer to area maps and rare books to identify abandoned or underused temples. At their meeting Subhash Kapoor asked Sanjeevi specifically for Chola era bronze idols, which Sanjeevi agreed to procure. It is thought that he even showed Subhash Kapoor photographs of some the temples and idols he would target. This was every dealer's dream come true. What Sanjeevi was offering was not one or two Chola bronzes but a templeful of them. Subhash paid Sanjeevi an advance for the idols and they agreed to meet again later that year. Meanwhile, Sanjeevi was to start making shipments of idols from his stock to prove that he could deliver on his 'contacts' and get these antiquities out of India and into Subhash's gallery in New York without a fuss.

Subhash probably could not believe his luck with the information and promise of services that Sanjeevi had made to him. He must have been happy to have met such a useful supplier. Even the grand old Deendayal, another of Subhash's long-time suppliers, wasn't as resourceful as this man.

Sanjeevi narrowed down on his target: the Sri Brihadeshwarar temple in Sripuranthan (not to be confused with Emperor Sri Rajaraja Chola's grand Brihadeeshwarar temple in Thanjavur). There was no reference to this temple in any prominent book or website. Sanjeevi had apparently been there a few times and knew that the dilapidated temple had not been under worship for over a decade (two, according to some accounts).

Sanjeevi recruited two local thugs, Rathinam and Kaliaperumal, via his old contact, the local art merchant Siva Kumar.

One night in January 2006, Rathinam and Kaliaperumal entered the temple by breaking open the lock and removed three of the eight bronze idols kept there. They glued the lever of the broken lock to make it appear as though nothing was amiss. The very next day Sanjeevi took the idols from them and paid them ₹2 lakh for their work. Not bad for a night's labour!

Sanjeevi exported the idols through Everstar International Services which belonged to his associate and right-hand man Packiakumar. The stolen gods were directly sent to Nimbus Import Export, Inc. in New York, which is owned by Subhash Kapoor.

In May 2006, Rathinam and Kaliaperumal raided the temple again using the same method and stole another three idols, for which they were again paid ₹2 lakh, and which were again exported directly to Subhash Kapoor by Sanjeevi.

The remaining two idols – an enormous, nearly four-foot-tall Nataraja (that Subhash would eventually sell to the NGA for $5.1 million) and a stunningly beautiful Lord Vishnu – were picked up in similar fashion. This operation required the participation of more foot soldiers owing to the size and weight of the idols. The thieves, however, demanded more money for this lot and were

Sripuranthan Nataraja

paid ₹3 lakh. And of course, again, these were exported, in November 2006, to Subhash Kapoor in New York from Chennai harbour.

Sanjeevi was paid a princely sum in dollars that was equal to ₹1,16,37,694 from Subhash Kapoor's HSBC Bank account in New York. Not a bad earning from a few lakhs of outlay that Sanjeevi had to make to his men on the ground.

Subsequently, Sanjeevi received another advance from Subhash Kapoor and the maps and old and rare books on Chola temples were put to use again. The next target that Sanjeevi identified was the Varadaraja Perumal temple in Suthamalli, just 10 km from Sripuranthan. Both villages are approximately 150 km inland from Puducherry. This temple was also in a state of disarray, opened only every three to four months for worship. As mentioned earlier, the gods from the Chola period Sundareshwarar temple had been relocated to the Varadaraja Perumal temple, which now housed a whopping eighteen idols.

Sanjeevi's gang of temple looters cleared out the temple over two days in February 2008. Sanjeevi Asokan took ten idols from the thieves for ₹25 lakh and sent them off to Subhash Kapoor – not directly this time but via Hong Kong and London. The remaining idols were sold off by the thieves to an unknown foreigner in an antique shop in Puducherry.

Sanjeevi's earnings from the heist? ₹1,01,10,418![4] And it was the Suthamalli Nataraja and Sivakami matched pair that Subhash Kapoor was flogging in March 2007, even before he had got physical possession of them. He was trying to sell them for $8.5 million, or approximately ₹34,00,00,000 in those days – a brilliant return on investment by any standard!

But here's the shocking part. It was only when the Suthamalli temple was opened on the Tamil New Year in 2008 – on 14 April, to be precise – that the theft was even discovered. Imagine everyone's shock when the temple doors must have swung open after months to reveal that the gods that had been there since the twelfth century had vanished. By then rates were being put on our priceless patrimony and they were being sold off in posh steak joints in New York. A case was registered in the Udayarpalayam police station that day. And it was only in June 2009 that the case was transferred to the Idol Wing.

The discovery of the theft in Sripuranthan was even stranger. After the Suthamalli heist was detected there was naturally concern about the Sripuranthan idols due to the proximity of the two villages which are just 10 km apart. According to the Idol Wing, in June 2008, two months after the Suthamalli theft was found out, a team of HR&CE department officials went to the Sripuranthan temple intending to shift the idols to an icon centre. 'But the villages restrained their process and promised to safeguard the idols by providing a new grille gate. After the grille gate was ready, on 18.08.2008, HR&CE officers, local police and the villagers tried to open the lock and found the lock was broken. Idols were stolen away.'[5] This means that when the officials visited the temple in June 2008 they didn't even open the temple to see if everything was all right. Instead a grill door was commissioned to protect the eleventh-century idols that had already been exported to the US two years earlier! The idols were all gone. The ruse that the thieves used – gluing the sawn-off lock back together to fool passers-by – clearly worked wonders and certainly managed to fool the HR&CE department officials and the villagers. A police case was registered and in due course transferred to the Idol Wing in November 2008.

And now the authorities didn't even have photos of the priceless idols they were on the hunt for. They had no clues, nor any idea that it was Sanjeevi and Subhash Kapoor's handiwork. Such was the state of affairs in Sripuranthan and Suthamalli.

3

The Container from Mumbai

Subhash Kapoor and Sanjeevi Asokan had been dealing in antiquities for decades before they were caught. The Suthamalli and Sripuranthan idols, which ultimately did them in, were just a drop in the ocean. Many, many more treasures had passed through their hands. So how come they never got caught all those years? Well, for one, Subhash had friends everywhere, and for another, he had the luck of the devil. Take for instance the case of 'the container from Mumbai'. That was quite a close call for Subhash.

In March 2007 in New York, Subhash Kapoor got a call that made him go numb. According to newspaper reports it was his 'contact', someone who worked in the Indian consulate in New York, warning him that the authorities in the US had been tipped off by their Indian counterparts about a container that was consigned to his company, Nimbus Import Export, Inc. Subhash's contact's warning was clear and precise – 'Stay away!'[1]

According to US Immigration and Customs Enforcement (ICE), the Indian authorities at the Jawaharlal Nehru Port Trust in Mumbai had become suspicious of a New York–bound shipment that was labelled as marble garden furniture.[2] For one, the shipment weighed tonnes – much more than what mere garden furniture could possibly weigh – and, secondly, the exporter was a garment and textile company, not a furniture manufacturer. These things set off alarm bells. In actual fact, the shipment contained $20 million worth of Indian art, some of it stolen, headed into Kapoor's hands.[3]

Dumping $20 million worth of goods was a heart-wrenching decision. But it had to be done. This was the cost of doing business. Kapoor immediately sent a message to his agent to abandon the shipment. Then he likely contacted his trustworthy associate, 'Shantoo', his saviour. Shantoo would sort out everything, go into damage control mode. After all, India was a land of compromises! And many ruffled feathers had to now be smoothened.

As Kapoor would have hung up, and put his phone into his pocket, had you been in the room, you would have seen his deformed right ear. He would later explain in his unpublished 'statement of voluntary confession' recorded by P. Ashok Natarajan, chief investigation officer, in the immediate physical presence of the Hon'ble Sub-Divisional Executive Magistrate Tr. James Chellaiah and a respectable local witness, Tr. Pandivarajan, 'During my childhood days I was kidnapped for ransom and was rescued by police near Haryana Rajasthan border. In this incident one of the kidnappers bit[e] off my right ear lobe and since then it was deformed.'

The newspapers in India announced the seizure of the goods in the US with screaming headlines and long reports. The *DNA* on Friday, 23 March 2007 reported, 'DRI helps US Customs bust antiques scam' and went on to describe the seizure:

> After a tip off from the Mumbai wing of the DRI [Directorate of Revenue Intelligence], the United States Customs authorities recently detained a multi-crore consignment of Indian antiques . . . some dating back to the 2nd century AD and 12th century AD . . .
>
> Ministry of External Affairs (MEA) would now have to step in if the rare antiques – sandstone sculptures of Lord Shiva and Parvati, a dancing Ganesha, Parvati with infant Ganesha and Kartikeya, a photo album belonging to an Indian king that was shot at London in the late 1800s, collectively worth crores of rupees – are to be brought back to India.
>
> Overall about 75 statues, paintings, silverware and antiquated photo albums have been detained by the US Customs authorities . . .
>
> The US based importer has been running this racket of selling such priceless historical artefacts since 1976.

The importer used to source the antiques from Indian temples and historical sites and ship them across to him in the USA.

The Indian authorities have identified the export house – Nimbus Imports and Exports.[4]

In an ideal world, this would have been an open-and-shut case. Kapoor should have been arrested then and there. *The Hindu* even reported that 'When ICE [US Immigration and Customs Enforcement] pounced on the consignment and brought Kapoor in for questioning, he apparently acknowledged being aware of the laws governing importation of cultural properties from India, and the fact that shipment could not be lawfully imported. Therefore, he elected to abandon the items.'[5] But still nothing happened. The case just fell through the cracks in the US. The agent in charge of the case didn't seem to want to move on it. All that was left were many questions that are still unanswered.

Why didn't the Indian authorities themselves stop the shipment at Mumbai?

Who made that warning phone call to Subhash Kapoor?

How did the caller have confidential information shared between the Indian authorities and US Customs?

And why was Kapoor allowed to continue his trade for years after this?

That Subhash Kapoor remained untouched goes to show what I said earlier: the man had friends and well-wishers in high places. And really good luck. But little did he know then that this abandoned container would eventually come back to haunt him.

Shortly after Subhash Kapoor got that warning call, he got busy. If the Mumbai–New York route was under watch, he had to find another way to get his shipments to America.

He had been using the Hong Kong route earlier, to get to New York the Ardhanarishvara idol that he later sold to the AGNSW in 2004 for $300,000. Now he asked his assistant to reactivate it by contacting their trusted associate Ms Lai Sheung at Union Link International Movers Ltd in Hong Kong. He once more planned to use the Chennai/Kolkata/Mumbai–Hong Kong route to get his hauls out of India and then ship the goods to New York via London. Here's how it worked: Lai Sheung would receive the shipment in Hong Kong, keep it for a while, and either directly send it on to Subhash in New York or sometimes send it to Neil Perry-Smith, an art restorer, in London who would then send it on to Subhash after a while.[6]

Why such a convoluted route? Because by keeping the idols in Hong Kong and London for a while he was able to create a layer, though only skin deep, of distance between the idols' recent home in India and the art gallery in New York. If anything, sending shipments directly from India to Subhash Kapoor was a risky thing to do. Also, if the movement of antiquities to the

US was being watched, by routing them through Hong Kong and London, the shipments may pass under the radar. Union Link is just one such company providing this service. There are many other specialized art movers who offer similar 'services'. Incidentally Union Link may be linked to other clandestine activities, including supplying goods to North Korea. The authorities are still investigating this.[7]

So how exactly did the nuts and bolts of Subhash Kapoor's back end work? Let's look at one instance of how Sanjeevi would keep him plied with fresh antiquities, and how these would be illegally shipped to the US. Around the time that Subhash Kapoor was doing the damage control after he abandoned his ill-fated March consignment to the US, he received an email with eleven attachments.

An extraordinary bronze loomed on his computer screen as he flipped through the images. The photos showed a fabulous Chola bronze – a thousand years old, standing in a dark, dirty room with the mudlines of termites clearly visible on the walls. Such photos of stolen idols sent by thieves to gallerists and dealers for sale are known in law enforcement circles as 'robber photos'.

Perhaps he walked up to his bookshelf, and picked out the three works he usually referred to – the bibles of his trade, heavily used and dog-eared, with innumerable tapes and notes stuck in them. These were *The Chola Temples* series by S.R. Balasubrahmanyam, *Early Cola*

Bronzes by Douglas Barrett and *Bronzes of South India* by P.R. Srinivasan. All three books had spectacular examples of idols from the same time period and it wasn't hard for him to find the pages which spoke of the Rishabhavahana: Lord Shiva with his matted hair, and snakes coiled around his head like a turban, resting his hand above the bull Nandi. The photos Subhash was sent indicated that it was a complete set, including the bull, covered with grime and layers of dust.

The photos in the email were not great, but he could still make out the ornamentation. The upper left hand of Shiva was broken, so was the upper right, but nothing that his friend in London could not fix.

In the email, which was later accessed by HSI, Sanjeevi asked him if he could send the two pieces he wanted that month itself because the preferred officials were on duty. The piece he had expected the previous month had still not reached him but was likely to be with him the following week. Meanwhile he had made a move for this huge piece (the Rishabhavahana) and had taken some photos. The piece was 48 inches high, weighed 140 kg (without the bull which was 26x30). He would get things moving once Subhash sent him an approval for the new piece.

It was all so simple! All Subhash had to do now was reply with a 'yes', transfer some money (not much as compared to the price of the items at the other end) and he would have a precious antique in his hands in New York. He would need to get it cleaned up – maybe this one had to go to Neil Perry-Smith in London for repair

– maybe give it some artificial patina, then find a reputed scholar to write a flowery catalogue. For a piece of this quality he could even do without the chemical analysis. Normally it is very difficult to carbon-date bronzes and the main idols were solid cast. The vahanas – the Nandi bull in this case – are usually hollow cast and could have a soft core. The casting method is such that there is a core of clay left inside the image. By dating the clay using thermoluminescence, one can establish the age of the sculpture.

He then needed to hunt down a hungry museum curator, throw in a few pichavais or broken terracottas as gifts, and he would have made hundreds of thousands in profit.

The temple that was targeted this time was the Sri Balambika-Karkodeswarar temple of Kamarasavalli, a village in Ariyalur district of Tamil Nadu, and a prime hunting ground for Subhash Kapoor, owing to his association with Sanjeevi Asokan's gang. It was an early Chola brick temple, converted to granite by the great monarch Sri Rajaraja Chola, and further enriched by donations from his famed son, Rajendra Chola. The temple was embellished with fantastic stone and bronze sculptures.

Sanjeevi Asokan was more resourceful and daring than Subhash's older suppliers. Shipping out priceless idols was child's play for him. He knew exactly how with the right connections you could hoodwink the whole system to pull off a remarkable stunt. Yes, it was really a stunt.

Kapoor's north Indian suppliers had to go through a set

procedure – one they had perfected from the 1970s when Indian law enforcement got wind of the diplomatic pouch route. Till then diplomats would use their immunity and guarantees against their luggage being inspected to spirit out Indian art. Now that that means was under suspicion, they had to find a decent enough craftsman, show him the photos of the intended product and get him to make a few similar-looking replicas. Then, through a front company registered as a handicrafts exporter with the local office of the Regional Handicrafts Development Commissioner, they had to get the shipment certified as newly made handicrafts by showing the photos of the replicas. Then, they had to deliberately under-declare the value of the consignment so that it could fly under the customs radar and avoid further checks. Of course, the critical step was to slip in the original in the forest of fakes at the time of shipping.

Alternatively, they would approach the regional Archaeological Survey of India (ASI) office, show them the same photographs of the replicas, as well as the replicas themselves, and secure a non-antiquity certificate. It helped that the exporter was required to bring the items to the ASI office for inspection, rather than the ASI official inspecting them at the time of shipping. A certificate, valid for 180 days, to export would then be given. In the deliberately undervalued export consignment, the genuine antique would, once again, be shipped off along with the replicas.

Sanjeevi's modus operandi was similar. However, of late he had been riding high on confidence and the complicity of more flexible officials meant that he just shipped the original antique instead of even bothering to hide it among fakes. Sanjeevi showed how easily this could be done when he shipped a Nataraja, an Uma and a Ganesha in May 2006.

The container freight station in north Chennai is where containers – the enormous steel boxes used in shipping – are loaded and then transported to the port. Even at night, it is always humid, dirty and hot. It was worse that May, when the famed Chennai heat coupled with power cuts to drive temperatures and tempers even higher. It was past 9 p.m., yet the area around the government loading facility was still teaming with activity, and the roadside eateries were dishing out an assortment of biryanis and chilli dosas. Since movement of container trucks inside city limits during the day was not allowed, they lined the roads for several kilometres at this time in a serpentine queue to pick up the loaded containers to transport them to the port. The shipping clerks, responsible for seeing through their employers' outgoing shipments, with their paper folders carrying an assortment of invoices, packing lists and shipping bills, rushed to the customs desk to get their shipping bills (mandatory documents to be filed by the exporter) passed.

It was a task so routine for the customs clerk, the government official who ensures all the paperwork for export is in order, that he hardly ever read through the contents of the bills presented to him. He had to just check on his computer screen if the shipping bill number showed up as assessed. The assessment takes place earlier at the customs head office, opposite the port, where they had already entered the exporter's name, commodity, packages and decided if the price mentioned in the shipping bill was reasonable for the commodity being shipped. The customs clerk's job was the next and most vital step – examination, which technically meant he had to randomly pick a bill and physically go and examine the cargo to see if it actually matched the items listed in the shipping bill. In reality, he got up only three times during a shift – once for coffee and twice for his cigarette. His hand stamped the red 'Examined' endorsement mechanically on every twentieth copy, and 'Let Export' on every shipping bill. The bills he cleared went into a huge box. He had to clear 250 such shipping bills every shift. A little inducement to bring the stamp down on the paperwork always helped him work faster, more cheerfully. So much for checks!

Sanjeevi's man (he cannot be named for operational secrecy reasons) took out his already soaked handkerchief to wipe the sweat on his forehead. He had argued with his boss that the risks were too high. Sanjeevi planned to send the idols as a loose shipment, not in a private container, which meant the crates containing the idols would be given to a shipping company as stand-alone items at a public loading area within the customs premises. The stakes were enormous as there are at least half a dozen other containers being loaded at the same time with over a hundred labourers and over a dozen customs officials hovering around. If something were to go wrong it would happen in front of everyone. A private container on the other hand could be loaded at Sanjeevi's warehouse, with a single customs officer watching – fewer people to 'manage'. He had pleaded with Sanjeevi to wait for a few months and collect more 'orders' and ship out as a full container so that they could bring the container to their godown. But his boss wouldn't listen. He had instructed him to wait till 9 p.m., which is when the customs officials changed shifts, and then tell him who was at the desk. His man called with the name. There would be no problem. He told him to proceed.

Sanjeevi's man looked at the documents once again. There were three items listed as 'Indian Handmade Artistic Handicraft Items' worth $1,500, which included $150 for the mandatory insurance. He checked again. There were three roughly nailed wooden crates – he had been with them on the truck from Mamallapuram, the sleepy Pallava heritage town, 65 km from Chennai. Though the documents listed the gross weight of the entire shipment as 225 kg, his boss had insisted he use a 3-tonne forklift to offload the crates from the truck and stack them in the loading yard. Not for any other reason than that he simply couldn't afford an accident such as the forklift dropping the crates in front of everyone and revealing their contents. All sides of the crates were marked 'Fragile'. He looked into the description once again and swallowed hard. He wanted no mishaps during the loading as there would be at least ten other men looking on to ensure their shipments were loaded safely into the same container.

Earlier in the morning, it had been a cakewalk at the

central customs office when the shipping bill was assessed. He was tense there as well, as the price on the invoice was much lower than even for poor quality steel, and this was bronze. Yet, his boss had been confident. He had all the necessary paperwork ready, including the faded blue colour photocopy of the certificate from the handicrafts promotion body. His boss had given him two envelopes, one marked *P* (photos) and the other unmarked. The officer sitting across the large wooden desk seemed to know which one to open. He took the one marked *P* and shook out the contents. Five grainy photos of Shiva as Nataraja, Uma and Ganesha fell on to the table. The other, fatter, envelope went right into the drawer. The same drawer yielded an assortment of blue and red seals and stamps, which he proceeded to put on the bills.

Now, in the evening, he had to get the shipping bill passed by the customs clerk. He needed the critical 'Let Export' stamp. The assessed shipping bill went, neatly tagged with twine, to the desk. The officer seemed irritated with the non-functional table fan as he saw the bunch of documents. There were no fat envelopes here. The shipping clerk called his boss and passed the phone to the customs officer. Into the phone, the officer said a four-digit number. Outside the customs facility, a Yamaha stopped near an auto, checked the licence plate – it had the same number that the customs officer had just said into the phone – and passed on a dirty bundle crudely wrapped in an old newspaper to the auto driver. The auto driver made a phone call to the same customs officer who then put the stamp, leaving a blue and a red barely legible stain on the paper and scribbled over it, 'Examined', 'Let Export'.

Most people had returned from their dinner and the container loading area was a hive of activity, with the crowd of people and forklifts desperately trying not to come in one another's way. Sanjeevi's man searched for the container to New York that they had chosen to use for the shipment. He finally found it parked in one corner, its bright orange sides shining in the floodlights. He passed the papers to the stuffing clerk and the forklift was put in motion again. In a cloud of dark diesel fumes, the three wooden crates were neatly stacked in one corner of the container. Quickly, the rest of the container was filled with the other cargo, consisting of an assortment of cardboard boxes with a myriad markings. The surveyor tallied the number of crates with the stuffing plan and signalled for the container to be closed and sealed. The blue doors closed smoothly across their rubber lining and the bottle seals clicked shut – one-time locks that ensured there were no keys – and would be broken only upon arrival at New Jersey, USA. Only then, after over five hours, did the shipping clerk breathe easy. He still felt they should have shipped the goods in a full container as their neighbour did for such shipments, loading the material right inside their godown in Mahabalipuram. His boss was just trying to save a few dollars.

The next day, Sanjeevi's man waited impatiently at the office of the shipping company they had used. It was past lunchtime by the time he got the bill of lading released. The bill of lading was a miracle document – a document of title, proof of receipt by the shipping company and evidence of the contract of carriage, all rolled into one. Of course, the foot soldier knew nothing about all this. All he knew was that he needed to ensure he had three originals and his boss would send them via courier to the consignee. The ultimate receiver had to show any one of the originals at the destination to the carrier's agent to take delivery of his goods.

He rechecked the shipper and consignee names.

Shipper: Everstar International Services (Packiakumar's company)
Consignee: Nimbus Export Import, Inc.

A few hours later, Sanjeevi's man got off the bus at the Tiger Cave stop in Mahabalipuram and hurriedly crossed the road as the sun went down. When he handed over the thick set of documents to Sanjeevi, he enquired about the 'shipped on board' date. The vessel would sail out of Chennai port the next day. Sanjeevi emailed a copy of the documents to the consignee, Subhash Kapoor.

The computer completed transmitting the message. He looked at the calendar on the wall, with the smiling face of Lord Murugan, the son of Lord Shiva and Parvati. Thursday, 11 May 2006.

'I have just sent your parents abroad!' he must have thought.

INVOICE

Exporter M/S EVERSTAR INTERNATIONAL SERVICES #11 D, OTHAVADAI STREET MAMALLAPURAM 603 104 INDIA	Invoice No& Dt 05/ 09-05-2006	Exporter's Ref I.E.C. 0405025041	
	Buyer's Order No & Date		
Consignee M/S NIMBUS IMPORT EXPORT INC # 2, CROSS FIELD AVENUE SUITE 105, WEST NYACK, NY 10994 USA	Buyer(if other than consignee)		
	Country of Origin of goods INDIA	Country of final Destination USA	
Pre-Carraige by	Place of Receipt by Precarrier	Terms of Delivery and Payment	
Vessel/Flight No BY SEA	Port of Loading CHENNAI/INDIA	DP	
Port of Discharge NEW YORK	Port of Delivery NEW YORK		

Marks & Nos/ Container No.	No & kind of Pkgs	Description of Goods	Quantity NOS.	Rate. USD	Amount USD
EIS 1 TO 5	5 W/CASE	INDIAN HAND MADE ARTISTIC HANDICRAFT ARTICLES			
		1. BRASS GANESH	1	150.00	150.00
		2. BRASS SIVA	2	350.00	700.00
		3. BRASS DEVI	2	250.00	500.00
			FOB 1350-		
		FREIGHT & INSURANCE			150.00
			FOB ₤ 1350-		

Amount chargable (In Words USDS ONE THOUSAND FIVE HUNDRED ONLY)				TOTAL	1,500.00
Declaration We declar that this invoice shows the actual price of the goods described and that all particulars are true and correct.			Signature & Date for EVERSTAR INTERNATIONAL SERVICES Proprietor		

Shipping invoice dated 9 May 2006

4

The Arrest

24 August 2008. While Sanjeevi Asokan had been busy running his ring of temple thieves for at least fifteen years, supplying to international big fish like Subhash Kapoor and growing fabulously rich in the process, most people knew him only as an art dealer of repute with a gallery in Parry's Corner in Chennai.

But the net was closing around him thanks to one of the heroes of our story: Deputy Superintendent of Police (DSP), Selvaraj, who had been working with the Idol Wing for eighteen months. Ironically, the Idol Wing is considered a punishment posting, not a plum and prestigious one. Since its founding in 1980, the Idol Wing of Tamil Nadu had become a depleted force within a decade of its establishment. It had lost its sheen and bite after the dedicated core who had championed its cause initially had either retired or been transferred to other departments. It became a parking ground for officers who had fallen out of favour with the government to cool their heels temporarily or rot there till retirement. By 2010, the Idol Wing had been reduced to just nine police personnel. It borrowed from other units when in need, even for basic search and seizure operations.

So bad was the state of the Idol Wing that in 2017 the Madras High Court censured the state government and seventeen police officers were assigned to the Idol Wing.

But we're getting ahead of ourselves. Back to 24 August 2008. It is important to remember the institutional constraints under which Selvaraj was working.

Selvaraj finally had information that could lead to Sanjeevi being caught red-handed taking possession of stolen idols, and being put behind bars. However, at that time the scale of Sanjeevi's operations was not known to Selvaraj. He didn't know he was the man behind the Sripuranthan and Suthamalli robberies, or that he would lead to Subhash Kapoor. Back then Sanjeevi was just another dealer running an illicit antiquities racket who was about to go down. Selvaraj was at Parry's Corner for this career-defining operation.

I spoke to a key member of Selvaraj's team about that day. It was a Sunday, the only day of the week that the roads around Parry's Corner revealed their true size. Selvaraj didn't remember ever noticing how wide they were. Even portions of the broken footpaths were visible. On weekdays, all you could see was people everywhere. He smiled as he spotted a person reverently tear off a poster of Rajinikanth, or Thalaivar as he's lovingly called. The movie *Kuselan* had bombed at the box office. In its place went up a rather stocky-looking

Jayam Ravi in a leather jacket – *Dhaam Dhoom* was to be released the coming week. It was past four in the evening and the Burma Bazaar shops were doing brisk business. He wondered if they were already making pirated copies of *Dhaam Dhoom*. It was surprising how talented human minds could also be so devious and crooked. But then he turned away from these thoughts. Today he was on the hunt of a lifetime. In fact, the culmination of an eighteen-month long search.

Though the initial information had been quite sketchy, the pieces of the puzzle slowly started to fall in place. Sanjeevi Asokan was believed to be in the Mannady locality of Chennai, just a stone's throw from Selvaraj's patrol jeep. The police's quarry, or prey – two middle-aged men – had boarded a bus three hours ago at Udayarpalayam, carrying a heavy gunnysack. There was further confirmation at the halfway toilet stop that the two gents had remained inside the bus. The hope was that they would lead him to Sanjeevi. All they had to do was follow them till they handed over the bag containing a stolen idol to their boss at the gallery. The police would then swoop in and arrest the lot.

He left his patrol jeep and got into an unmarked white Ambassador – a hired taxi. He remembered his discussion in the morning with his seniors. They were still not convinced of his plan. He had shown them all the cellphone transcripts, played a few of the recordings. It was plain for everyone to see that a major sale was about to happen and this was their chance to catch Sanjeevi. But still they had debated for an hour. Typical slow government. He was under pressure since time was running out. He stepped out for a cigarette. He had no choice; this was too big a chance to miss and it was time to play his trump card. He called G. Thilakavathi, Additional Director General of Police.

The conversation was brief. She asked him if he was sure. 'Madam, we are currently tracking a total of fifty-three SIM cards and fifteen mobile IMEI (a unique serial number that all mobile phones have) numbers tagged to the racket,' he informed her. Things happened pretty quickly after that.

He split his eight men into three teams. The quarry would most likely take a rickshaw from the bus stand to the gallery. Traffic was light and his teams would move in as soon as they went into the meeting with Sanjeevi. The trap was set.

Then it happened.

'Sir, there was a call and they are getting down at Wallajah Road.' This was from the team which was tapping the mobile phones.

'Why?'

'He said they will meet at Nair Mess for lunch instead.'

Something was amiss. It was 4.30 p.m. already – why was there a sudden change of plan?

'Sir, silver Qualis moving towards you.' This was Sanjeevi's car.

Selvaraj signalled his driver to follow the Qualis. The other two teams rushed towards the new venue via a different route.

But the Qualis managed to shake Selvaraj off its trail.

He realized he had lost the chance to arrest the boss. Now he had to take a call. He hesitated for a moment, before asking the driver to turn towards Nair Mess. He looked at the red façade of the Madras University building, his face matching its colour. He had come close to busting the racket so many times before. But now he knew for sure. Someone had leaked the information about the trap at the last minute – again. Who could it be? Only a handful of very senior people knew about the operation.

At Nair Mess, the heavy gunnysack stood out like a sore thumb. The two men, Rathinam and Siva Kumar, would be easy pickings. He was tempted to wait and see if the Qualis would come, but his gut told him he were looking at another failure. His anger turned on the two in front of him. Throwing caution to the wind, he got down and banged the car door shut.

The other two vehicles arrived with their sirens on.

The two stood stunned, like deer caught in headlights, before they bolted. The fools didn't factor the weight of the bag. Within minutes both had been handcuffed.

The gunny bag landed in the boot of the Ambassador with a loud metallic clink. As they cut the twine, the bag opened, revealing a dirty yet beautiful bronze Amman, a female deity.

The operation was not a success, yet they did bag something. In the mandatory press release, DSP Selvaraj held back the information about the big fish that got away.

Selvaraj had to bide his time until he got his next opportunity which presented itself after a few months.

By then the two men who had been caught had

happily ratted on their boss. They confirmed that Sanjeevi Asokan was running a ring of idol thieves and smugglers, something Selvaraj already knew. But then they mentioned two particular robberies they had carried out – at the temples in Suthamalli and Sripuranthan – and it became apparent to Selvaraj that Sanjeevi in fact ran the largest idol smuggling network in south India with his tentacles spread across many states. Selvaraj knew he had to try again to get his man. He knew where he lived, even which school his daughter went to. They had marked his offices in Chennai, Mamallapuram and Puducherry and his 'resort' in Kodaikanal. He had a list of Sanjeevi's relatives, across the state, in Kochi. His concern was the close escapes. Even the most meticulously planned operations had failed due to last-minute glitches – too many to be just coincidences. There had to be a black sheep, a mole in the department. But who?

In March 2009, a chance intercept revealed Sanjeevi's plans of vanishing forever, once the school exams got over in a few days. Perhaps he had caught wind of the confession of his foot soldiers, Rathinam and Siva Kumar, naming him and his exploits. The police no longer needed to catch him red-handed. They had witnesses against Sanjeevi. They had, at best, only a few days before he would be lost forever, reduced to occasional blips in Bihar, Madhya Pradesh, Odisha or, even worse, escape and go out of the country altogether, with fifteen mobile phones, fifty-three SIM cards and the unseen hands (and many homes) helping him. But Sanjeevi's luck was about to run out.

The warrant took forty-eight hours to come through. Selvaraj knew that a visit to Sanjeevi's home would be a waste. A locked house greeted the team. The silver Qualis was still parked there. His mind was racing in every direction. Finally, hope came from a taxi call centre. There was a booking for the domestic airport. The flight manifests were scanned and thirty minutes later, he had the answer – Sanjeevi was headed to Kochi.

This time Selvaraj decided to trust no one except his immediate team. They left by road and drove through the night to Kochi. Protocol required that he inform the local police in Kochi – after all, the Tamil Nadu Idol Wing had limited manoeuvrability in another state. It was 5 a.m. The warrant would have to be handed over to the Kerala authorities but he still had a few hours before that needed to be done. Selvaraj hoped the operation would be over long before that.

Another call. He dreaded who it might be, but it was the best news he could have hoped for. He had an address. The months he had invested in cultivating his informants had finally yielded gold!

They parked a few blocks away and walked towards the multi-storeyed hotel. He had to be sure that Sanjeevi was inside. But he had an ace up his sleeve. He stopped at the tender coconut stand by the pavement. A few deft cuts by the sharp knife – the refreshing liquid calmed his nerves. As he paid the vendor, came the words he actually wanted to hear, 'Yes sir! He just returned after his morning walk. He is inside.'

He had to act on the go-ahead right away. He called

the one person he knew he could trust – Additional DGP Thilakavathi. The answer was quick and short. He had her permission to move in before informing the local police.

The team quickly fanned out. The smell of spices from the breakfast being prepared pervaded the lobby and competed with the scent of jasmine. What audacity to book the room in his own name! The register read – Arrival: Monday 20 March [2009]. Native: Chennai. Stay: 2 days. Purpose: Sightseeing. Allotted: 11th floor.

Selvaraj signalled for the phones to be taken off the hook and left a man to ensure that no calls were made from the reception to Sanjeevi's room tipping him off. Two men guarded the entry and exit of the hotel. He had just three men with him now. The lift arrived on the eleventh floor with a loud 'ting'. The men quickly positioned themselves against the door, one on each side, as he rang the bell.

He couldn't believe his luck. Sanjeevi himself answered the door!

The next few minutes passed in a blur. Charges and countercharges were hurled. He had not expected to see so many people inside the room so early in the morning. The raiding team was outnumbered two to one. Phone calls flew, and from what he heard of the one-sided conversations, they were all to important people. He decided this was getting nowhere. Given time, the fellow might be able to access someone high enough who may give inconvenient orders. The arrest was made then and there.

A full contingent of Kerala Police assembled and escorted Selvaraj, his team, and his prized catch back into

Tamil Nadu. They stopped for breakfast at Coimbatore and it finally hit him. They had done the impossible. They had the kingpin!

Their good fortune continued. They received approval to book Sanjeevi under the Goondas Act, instead of just the Indian Penal Code (IPC) sections 380 (theft) and 457 (house trespass and house-breaking by night), making the offence non-bailable. So now he would be available to them for questioning, and couldn't just disappear.

But then came some shocking news. The computers they had seized from the hotel room drew a blank. Their hard disks had been wiped clean. Selvaraj was stunned. From the time the door of the hotel room had opened, he had kept a hawk's eye on the computers. He decided to send the hard disks to the National Informatics Centre (NIC) in Delhi to try to recover something at least. But two weeks later, the response from the NIC was discouraging. The hard disks were empty. It was impossible to retrieve any data from them. Had Sanjeevi been tipped off again?

After the arrest, several stolen idols were recovered from Sanjeevi's possession. Though it was known that Sanjeevi had been involved in an international idol smuggling operation, and there was even talk of retrieving stolen idols from foreign countries, there was no reference to Subhash Kapoor in any of the statements by the police or the arrested persons.

We now turn to an unpublished extract from the
confession of Subhash Kapoor that illuminates his and
Sanjeevi's relationship in Kapoor's own words:

My name is Subhash Chandra Kapoor, Age 63/2012, S/o.
Parshothan Ram Kapoor and my mother is Shashi Kapoor
. . . The Sub-divisional Executive Magistrate explained
to me that I am not bound to make any confession as per
Indian Law and if I do, it would go against me during
trial. I understand, but still I wish to disclose what had
happened truly . . .

I visit India, Pakistan, Hong Kong, Thailand, Bangkok,
Afghanistan, Sri Lanka, Cambodia. I visited Tamil Nadu,
India, during May and July 2005 and May, September and
December 2006. I always stayed in Taj Connemara Hotel,
Chennai. But, I had given false Nationality as 'Indian' with
false address as 93, Bhulabhai Desai Marg, Mumbai – 69,
by suppressing my US Passport and my US Address. During
my such visits to Chennai, Mr. Sanjivi Ashokan of 'Arcelia
Gallery', Pitachaimani, Marichamy and Packiakumar
become my business contacts, commission agents and dealers
for whom I promised lucrative returns for supply of century
old Chola bronze idols and we visited some temples in Tamil
Nadu and Kerala. Sanjivi Ashokan already sent a bunch of
photos by post to my Art of the Past and some of them via
e-mail. I and Sanjivi Ashokan were in frequent telephonic
contacts. Sanjivi Ashokan's Cell Phone Number: 9382183***
Phone Number is 044-28510*** and 044-28550***.

5

The Emerald Linga Provides the Clue

Selvaraj was a frustrated man. In spite of catching the key offender, he was not sure if adequate punishment could be given to him. The applicable law of Tamil Nadu didn't help. He hesitated to file the final charge sheet on Sanjeevi. The reason? An amendment by Tamil Nadu in 1993 of Section 380 of the IPC.

The original section was:

> Whoever commits theft in any building, tent or vessel, which building, tent or vessel is used as a human dwelling, or used for the custody of property, shall be punished with imprisonment of either description for a term which may extend to seven years, and shall also be liable to fine.

To this the Tamil Nadu legislature added a subsection in 1993 that read:

Whoever commits theft in respect of any idol or icon in any building used as a place of worship shall be punished with rigorous imprisonment for a term which shall not be less than two years but which may extend to three years and with fine which shall not be less than two thousand rupees:

Provided that the court may, for adequate and special reasons to be mentioned in the judgment impose a sentence of imprisonment for a term of less than two years.

This amendment still stands. And means that under Section 380 someone who steals from a house can get a seven-year prison term, but stealing from a place of worship gets a maximum of three years and a fine of ₹2000!

Section 457 is more stringent and reads as follows:

Whoever commits lurking house-trespass by night, or house-breaking by night, in order to the committing of any offence punishable with imprisonment, shall be punished with imprisonment of either description for a term which may extend to five years, and shall also be liable to fine; and, if the offence intended to be committed is theft, the term of the imprisonment may be extended to fourteen years.

In June 2015, Prateep V. Philip, Additional Deputy General (ADG) of Tamil Nadu Police, then in-charge of the Economic Offences Wing, under which the Idol

Wing functions, was candid about what needed to be done to stem idol theft and highlighted a crucial flaw in our system. When asked what the greatest threats to our antiquities are, he said:

'The real threat is from the growing crime of idol theft and burglary. Inconsequential and weak legislations ... For example, trial is held for 7 years but the sentence imposed for the offences under sections 380 [theft] and 457 [house-trespass by night and house-breaking by night] IPC is 6 months. The offence of temple lock breaking followed by lurking criminal trespass by night in order to commit an offence of theft entails a maximum sentence of 14 years as per section 457 IPC. Since 1947, no offence of idol theft was ever visited with a sentence of 14 years, because penal law provides discretion to the punishing magistrate to impose lesser punishment of even 6 months for the same offence under Section 457 IPC.'[1]

So all of Selvaraj's efforts would probably only lead to a token sentence. Even in Selvaraj's best-case scenario Sanjeevi would likely be out of prison in no time.

But mysterious are the ways of God and fate. Just when they were losing hope, Selvaraj's team picked up a lead in October 2009 – the possible movement of a high-value item, unconnected to the Sanjeevi Asokan case. That operation would result in the Idol Wing gaining vital information that helped them turn the screws further on Sanjeevi Asokan, and so move one step closer towards nabbing Subhash Kapoor. Slowly but surely, thanks to these series of fortunate events, the dots would connect Subhash to Sanjeevi and the Suthamalli and Sripuranthan robberies.

Selvaraj was also itching to find out who the mole in the Idol Wing was. So he sent his deputy, Kader Batcha, to head the operation. He knew he was taking a big risk but he had to know for sure. With Kader Batcha in possession of crucial operational information, would the mission go as planned? Or would the Idol Wing be facing an uncannily lucky adversary yet again? This would be the biggest bust for them in decades, yet Selvaraj stayed home. He just wanted to see if the raid would be successful or not.

It was 26 October 2009. The heat was unbearable even at dusk. The dust from the hundreds of buses revving up combined with the sweat of the multitudes of people crowding at the terminus made it worse. The process of laying storm-water drains had cut open the roads, throwing the debris into the open drains, clogging them. A keen pair of eyes scanned every part of the facility. There was no sign of the quarry. Kader Batcha,[2] a light-skinned man with salt-and-pepper hair and a moustache, and a round, full face, was fidgety and he probably lit a cigarette to calm his nerves. Did his boss suspect him, he must have wondered?

It would be dark soon and difficult to profile the

multitudes transiting through the Chennai Mofussil Bus Terminus in Koyambedu. Luckily, the crowds were thinner than usual that Monday evening. He had four of his team members with him on this hunt, for the information was from a credible source. There was one person each at the entry and exit gates. One was standing on top of the bus at bus bay 44. The fourth was with him. Batcha carried his service revolver discreetly tucked beneath the Zam Zam blue belt. He had to make a strong case for bringing it along, but hoped he wouldn't need to pull it out. The Deputy Inspector General of Police (DIG) had made it pretty clear – use it only as a last resort. Any confusion in this crowd could easily result in a stampede.

He had planned the whole operation over the weekend. The mug shots sent by the Valangaiman (a panchayat town in Thiruvarur district of Tamil Nadu) station were grainy. He was looking for two suspects today – both under thirty, Hindu youth.

His mobile vibrated and he scanned the faces around him before he answered. It was his support team from the control room. The mobile phone tracker had just come on and it had been picked up by the Koyambedu tower. Target 1 was at the bus stand. Good that he had brought his weapon, he thought. This was no petty thief – he had earlier been arrested in a case of burning a police jeep. They were tracking thirteen SIM cards belonging to these persons. How people managed to procure so many despite the need to show identity and address proofs for getting one, was a mystery.

Another call from the control room. Another phone

tracker picked up by the same tower. Target 2, another jailbird recently out of Trichy prison, had reached. It was time for the team to act. He called the other three on foot to close in.

He scanned the crowd to try and identify his targets. Then he saw Target 1. There was something odd about him, something inconsistent. He tried to figure out what it was that alerted him. Probably just years of training. From the distance, he could not get a clear view of his face. The youth was dragging a gas cylinder. It appeared empty. He had no other luggage or bags. Then he saw the second fellow, standing a few feet away. There was no eye contact between the two, but the second man was looking at the cylinder a bit too frequently. Batcha had his quarry marked out. He signalled to his team and moved in. Within seconds, he had two men blocking off the sides. It had to be now.

He walked briskly towards the man with the cylinder. He dropped the cigarette he had lit earlier as he neared him. Another five steps and he would be on him. Their eyes met and he knew he had his man. He called out the name – Ramesh! The youth was too stunned to react. His accomplice realized something was amiss and made a mad dash towards the exit. He never saw the tackle coming. The wind was knocked out of him by the knee that hit his stomach and Senthil lay sprawled on the ground. Ramesh made no effort to fight back. He knew the game was over.

The cylinder was innovative. It had a screw-on lid. Inside it was a small bag. The light inside the police jeep was not too bright so he moved out of the jeep to inspect the contents of the bag against the headlights. The bag was not heavy and he gingerly reached in to pull out a parcel wrapped in newspaper. The weight appeared to be less than a kilo.

Placing it on the bonnet, he was about to tear off the newspaper when he noticed it was in Malayalam. He sniffed at the package and smelt paint.

Once he had got rid of the newspaper, he looked at the black object. He looked around and spotted a petrol station not too far away, walked up and showed his ID. The plastic bottle of petrol came quickly.

He washed the object with the petrol and smiled as the paint washed off, leaving a black mess on the ground. He called DSP Selvaraj immediately.

'We have the Maragatha Lingam – the Emerald Lingam!'

By the time he reached his office in Guindy, news had spread and his phone had been ringing constantly. For this was the first. There were still five unsolved cases of missing Emerald Lingams in Tamil Nadu. In addition, there was pressure from the neighbouring state of Kerala for another one stolen from the Kalady Sankara Math. Batcha had to prepare for the debriefing and the press conferences the next day. TV and newspaper reporters would all be there. He already knew what the headlines would be. 'Temple theft solved: Emerald Lingam worth 53 crore recovered'. This one had been stolen from the Maruntheeswarar temple at Thiruthuraipoondi in Thiruvarur district.

He didn't know where the others were. The seven

precious lingams were believed to bring anyone who worshipped them together and performed abhiseka (the ritual washing of a sacred object or image) on them, with boons ranging from immortality to Ambani-ish wealth. He smiled, thinking how he had given one a petrol abhiseka!

His head was still spinning as he started writing his report. As soon as he was done, he sent it to his boss, DSP Selvaraj, and to the Idol Wing.

Selvaraj was pleased, but he was also puzzled. The operation had been successful. Kader Batcha had sensitive operational information, the mission had been a triumph, there had been no leak. So who, then, was the black sheep inside the department?

The Emerald Lingam bust was on every news channel at prime time. Kerala Police picked up the news and next morning their officers reached Chennai. They were under great pressure to trace their own Emerald Lingam missing from the Kalady temple.

Earlier, on 27 March of that year, the half-foot Sivalinga, made of green stone believed to be emerald, went missing from the Adi Sankara Janmabhoomi temple at Kalady in Ernakulam district. Soon after this burglary, the state police had created a Temple Theft Investigation Special Team (TTIST) in 2009 which was successful in cracking many other cases.

The missing linga had been brought from the Sringeri Math in 1910 and was believed to be more than 500 years old. But investigators could not find any authentic document to date it. Some silver utensils used in the temple and the collection box at the tomb of Saradamba, mother of Adi Sankara, were also stolen along with the emerald linga.

The Kalady linga continues to elude the police to this day and, in fact, one more emerald linga was stolen in October 2016 from the Thiyagaraja Swamy temple in Thirukkuvalai in Tamil Nadu.

But here's what the Idol Wing learnt from the Kerala Police. They got their hands on a dossier on a small Ganesha the Kerala Police had seized from a truck driver earlier that year who had been involved in thefts from the two temples in Sripuranthan and Suthamalli.

It was one of the regular checkpoints that dot Kerala highways. The never-ending line of trucks inched their way up the steep incline, like a line of ants. The slight drizzle added to their slack pace as their tyres churned up the mud, due to the road widening work, into a slush. The only redeeming feature was the hot pazhampuri – ripe banana fritters – and thick tea, so unique to Kerala, that came in from the thatched-roof shop close by. The 'cleaners' riding the trucks were aware of the ritual – as the drivers slowed down before pulling over to stop, the cleaners would jump out with their papers and permits. Once in a while, when they were really bored, the traffic cops would get up and inspect the vehicle. Else, it was routine fair.

One particular truck seemed to slow down, but did not stop. Was the driver having trouble with his gearbox? Instinctively, the constable got up, swinging his lathi. His eyes locked with those of the driver for a second.

The driver panicked. Next minute, all hell broke loose. The truck screeched to a halt, the door opened and the driver sprinted off, heading for the thick bushes up the small hill. The constable let out a warning in Malayalam as he set off in pursuit. It was a short chase. In the slushy ground, the driver didn't make it to even ten feet away from the road before he slipped and fell flat on his face. He lay there helplessly, as he was handcuffed and then taken to the nearby police station.

An hour later, the wireless crackled in the control room. It was an important message for the TTIST.

The driver had in his possession a small Ganesha bronze idol. An hour later, he had revealed a lot, including his involvement with a large gang responsible for the raiding of two temples in Sripuranthan and Suthamalli. He had retained the small Ganesha idol from that loot. He told the Kerala Police that ever since he took the idol, he had been facing many problems. He had frequent punctures and the steering wheel did not turn properly. He probably believed the theft had brought him bad luck. And then he recorded the final submission – the idols were looted under the planning of Sanjeevi Asokan.

The Kerala Police recorded all this in their file and sent out a note to their counterparts in Tamil Nadu. Sadly, it had never reached Selvaraj, possibly due to the mole in the Idol Wing. The file simply got buried. But now he had this evidence in his hands and he could put it to good use. Very good use. The net was slowly closing around Sanjeevi and the screws were tightening. There was evidence, corroboration and even physical proof piling up.

Confronted with this information, and with the recent developments, he could sense Sanjeevi Asokan was within days of singing like a canary in the Trichy prison. The emerging details were unambiguously linking him to the Sripuranthan and Suthamalli robberies. The highlight of his song? The involvement of a foreigner in the racket. Subhash Kapoor. But Subhash Kapoor was sitting pretty in the US. While it was one thing to net Sanjeevi on home soil, getting Subhash Kapoor would be a whole new ball game.

6

Indy Takes Charge

As things were heating up for the idol smugglers in India, on the other side of the globe, in New York, a new posting occurred in 2009 in the office of the Homeland Security Investigations (HSI) department of US Immigrations and Customs Enforcement. It was time for the net to start closing in on Subhash Kapoor in the US.

In a nondescript city block in New York sat the new officer who took charge at ICE – often seen wearing his signature baseball cap bearing the initial *B*. It was the start of a single-minded pursuit to fight not just India's battle against looting of its cultural treasures but every source country's – Italy, Iraq, Pakistan, Cambodia. For the next eight years, his 5x5 office became the very nerve centre of the global struggle, spearheaded by the US, to clamp down on the growing trade in illicit antiquities. His appointment set in motion a series of events which will be covered in the rest of this book. Let us call him Indy – for security and operational secrecy reasons his identity cannot be revealed. A tall and lean history buff with a shaved head who was once a competitive swimmer and is a skilled pianist.

As he got to work, one of the first things that came up was that 2007 container from Mumbai. The shipment that Subhash Kapoor had abandoned. It wasn't amusing that a container load of Indian antiquities seized in 2007 was sitting right under his nose. He decided to reopen the case, and with that, unbeknown to Subhash, and the Indian authorities, the heat got turned up on him in the US.

The world of international art crime worked more like a photo-op and a PR agency. They seized a few artefacts, did some basic paperwork, held an embassy event where diplomats cheered one another under the glare of flashlights – and then nothing. No arrests, no prosecutions, no stiff penalties. The art market and dealers looked at these token seizures more as a cost of doing business. Anyway, the news hardly made it to the inside pages of newspapers even in the home countries. Where was the deterrent? No adverse publicity, no jail time, no major fines.

A case in point was a Pala period statue of Varaha, Vishnu in his boar avatar, rescuing the earth from the demon Hiranya. The ninth-century idol was beautifully adorned with carvings of all the ten incarnations of Lord Vishnu. It was stolen from the Varaha temple in Mandsaur, Madhya Pradesh, in 2000. Although it was later found in the possession of Namkha Dorjee who owned a gallery called Bodh Citta which he operated from his flat in New York, nobody was arrested. Dorjee apparently voluntarily handed over the statue to ICE once the agency was on to him.[1] Because of the absence of appropriate evidence the robbery could not be traced to anyone. The good news was that the idol was eventually returned to its home in the Mandsaur temple.

Evidence to build a foolproof case was still missing – evidence to prove that the US dealers were knowingly importing fresh loot from source countries in direct contravention of national and international laws, and then cooking up fake provenances to sell the antiquities to museums and collectors.

Indy looked up the original importer's name for the 2007 shipment – Nimbus. After some digging around he was more than interested in this particular importer. The 2007 event had hastened the pace of inbound shipments to Nimbus, not deterred them. There were parcels, couriers, containers, airfreight from India, Hong Kong, and the UK, and also from Thailand, Dubai and Nepal.

A key breakthrough was achieved when a small-time buyer of Subhash Kapoor's received a suspicious shipment in California. On being questioned, he pleaded guilty to customs violations, but was not prosecuted. He would be the small fish that led to the big fish. He was cultivated and soon became known as Informant 1, the first unnamed cooperating witness in the HSI's case against Subhash Kapoor. Over the next few years, Informant 1 wore a wire whenever he met Kapoor.

The next breakthrough was a shipment to Nimbus that came from London. It was from one of the most reputed art restorers, Neil Perry-Smith. The consignment had originated in Hong Kong. The paperwork for the goods was blatantly incorrect and there was a clear prima facie case for seizure. The shipment contained a bronze Buddha seated on a lion throne and two more tenth-century bronzes from India.

But no seizure was made. To find out how large was the spread of these activities, Indy decided to lie low, let this case be, in order to quietly follow Kapoor's modus operandi and track how he offered these goods for sale.

By early 2010, Indy was blown away by the extent of Subhash Kapoor's exploits. There were tons of shipments coming in by ocean containers, airfreight and courier parcels, making a mockery of international laws and customs regulations. But for the outside world Kapoor was hailed as a connoisseur, his objects were on loan at premier hotel lobbies, his gifts adorned prestigious museums, and he was invited for giving talks over cocktails and canapes to the elite on art and collecting.

Behind this façade was a veritable factory churning out paperwork for fake provenance, a plethora of assistants sending out portfolios to museums worldwide and a team of celebrated scholars writing catalogues and authenticating the items. He had a running account with the largest art auction houses like Sotheby's and Christie's and, above all, had all his objects vetted by the Art Loss Register (ALR) – a certificate which washed his tainted objects and gave them authenticity. The ALR is a privately run database of lost and stolen artefacts. If an item does not appear on the ALR it certainly does not mean it's clean. All it means is that it's not in the register – I know this sounds circular but that's what it is. (More about the ALR in Appendix 2.)

As the Kapoor dossier grew, Indy searched for support from India, both within the law enforcement agencies and outside. He needed evidence that Subhash Kapoor knowingly imported stolen antiquities and for that Indy needed to connect him to the original thefts. But when he tried reaching out to the Indian law enforcement agencies, he met with the same red tape that had derailed many previous investigations.

Undeterred, he continued to build his case and waited for the right time. Around 2011, he found help from four independent sources – Jason Felch, an American journalist, Michaela Boland, an Australian investigative reporter, Dr Kirit Mankodi, an Indian academic from Mumbai, and me, S. Vijay Kumar, an Indian shipping executive by day and blogger by night from Singapore.

Each of us was publicly active on the issue of cracking down on the international illicit trade in antiquities, running blogs and writing for newspapers. We were peers who used to follow each other's work and we naturally gravitated towards one another.

Jason is an award-winning author and investigative reporter and had spent a decade researching the illicit antiquities trade, particularly focusing on Italian antiquities and the complicity of big auction houses and big-ticket collectors in art smuggling.

In 2006, Jason Felch and Ralph Frammolino were shortlisted for the Pulitzer Prize in Investigative

Reporting for exposing the role of the J. Paul Getty Museum and other American museums in the black market for looted antiquities. Their book on the subject, *Chasing Aphrodite*, was a bestseller and has won heaps of awards. They continued to follow the issue on their blog chasingaphrodite.com.

Through Jason I got to know Michaela, currently the national arts, culture and entertainment reporter for ABC's Specialist Reporting Team. A former national arts reporter with the *Australian*, and Australia correspondent with entertainment industry bible *Variety*, Michaela's investigations into looted artefacts at the NGA would lead to an overhaul of collecting practices at Australian institutions.

Then there was Dr Mankodi. A rare academic, Dr Mankodi, is kind and accessible – more than what can be said of most other elitist experts – and has the energy of someone half his age when it comes to archaeology. He is the author of several books on Indian temples and their architecture. When he isn't teaching or writing books, he is busy working on his website – plunderedpast.com where he essentially does what the custodians must be doing – putting up cases of theft from archaeological sites and sending out notices and letters to various authorities.

And as mentioned earlier, I am a shipping executive by profession, but in 2007–08 I began blogging on Indian temple art and iconography on my website poetryinstone.in which continues to be an obsession. It was a kind of dummies' guide to understanding sacred art. Basically, I was putting out in the public domain my layman's approach to understanding sculpture and iconography. My blogs were free of technical and scholarly jargon and backed by photos and illustrations. My readers welcomed the information and would push me daily for new posts.

Once I attempted to deconstruct the iconic ardhanari form – the glorious duality of an androgynous Shiva, having given up half of his own self for his better half, Parvati. For a sculptor, to depict the concept was an iconographic nightmare, to balance the muscular male form with the sinuous grace of the female form in triple flexion – the famed tribhanga in Indian art, where the knee, waist and neck bend in alternating directions to create a gentle S shape in the body. I studied countless examples of this form in Indian art, from Elephanta to hundreds of early Chola temples. The sculptors found a unique way to bring balance to the otherwise unbalanced composition – the male form on the right, the female on the left, with the additional height of the male side causing it to tilt to the right. The master sculptors managed to offset this on the lower portion by bending the right leg, but the upper torso was still tilting awkwardly to the right. Masterfully, they brought in Shiva's vahana, the bull Nandi, into the picture upon which Shiva rests his arm to balance out the composition. This was the case in 99 per cent of the samples I studied. In a few rare examples, the male and female forms were switched from right to left. In such instances, the position of the bull was also changed. It was a post well received.

During the course of the study, I chanced on a

personal favourite. A Chola ardhanarishvara kosta (niche) stone sculpture from the Vriddhagisvarar temple in Vriddhachalam. Though the town was close to my native village, I hadn't been there for a decade. The images I used came from various archives, including the Huntington online archive, and from textual references. Why it became my favourite was because the sculpture had lost both its lower arms, yet its beauty and grace remained. The picture went up on my blog. Little did I know then that this post would be a game changer in the war against trafficking of sacred objects from India. But more on that later. For now suffice it to say that by 2011 our 'team' against art theft and smuggling would come together.

7

Revenge of a Spurned Lover

Around a year before I started my blog poetryinstone.
in, Joan Cummins, curator of Asian Art at the Brooklyn
Museum, posted a blog on 14 August 2007 titled
'Purchasing a major work of art for the collection'.

Cummins, who had been a museum curator for some
eight-odd years, wrote eloquently about that part of
her job that presented 'the headiest mixture of fun and
stress': acquiring new objects for the museum's collections.
According to her, the most critical metric of success in
buying art was not whether the director of the museum
or the critics or the discerning public liked the object.
No, Cummins said that the 'most pressing question,
when suggesting a potential purchase, is ... "will my
successors twenty or one hundred years from now like it?"'
Thankfully, she said, the curator is assisted in purchases
by an entire establishment of people, committees and
protocols 'to make sure that the institution stands behind

every new acquisition'. Cummins went on to describe
the acquisitions process through one object that the
museum had recently bought: a bronze two-foot-tall
Chola era sculpture of Lord Shiva made in circa 970
CE. An enthusiastic Cummins stated, 'This sculpture is
extremely rare, of a date and quality that simply does not
appear on the market anymore. And that is precisely the
sort of object that we were looking for.'[1]

If only museum curators fully understood the
devastating cost of their insatiable hunger for 'extremely
rare' art.

A series of subsequent blog posts gave some significant
insights into how museums acquire objects. One of the
major issues that curators and acquisitions committees
have to grapple with is authenticity, as per Cummins.
Especially since the sky-high prices of Asian art (fuelled
in no small measure by museums) have encouraged an
underground industry devoted to the creation of fakes.
Another major issue is provenance, or 'where the object
has been', as Cummins put it. In a searingly honest
appraisal, Cummins says, 'Most American museums once
participated in phases of happy-go-lucky acquisitiveness,
and they once subscribed to imperialist notions that
Western collectors were "rescuing" artefacts from
developing countries.'

But that's where the honesty ends. All this is in the
past, according to Cummins. 'Today, museums know that
they must serve as models of good collecting behaviour
- if there's nothing clean on the market, then you don't

buy anything, even if it would be fun to tout a new acquisition.'

If only that were true.

Cummins says for museums the ideal object is one that left its country of origin roughly in the middle of the twentieth century and one that has been sitting in someone's home or in a gallery since. Why? Because around the 1970s several countries enacted laws that prohibited the export of objects that are over 100 years old. Museums want to buy art that is on the right side of that Lakshman Rekha. 'Ideally, one can get written documentation of the object's recent history – the original bill of sale, maybe, or an old exhibition catalogue with an image of the piece. Unfortunately for museums, this sort of documentation adds enormously to an object's monetary value ... good provenance also offers a degree of reassurance about the authenticity of the object, because people weren't making as many forgeries in the early 20th century as they are today (they were making some, but often not very well).'[2]

Coming back to the Chola Shiva the museum had acquired, Cummins said: 'Brooklyn's Shiva has provenance back to the mid-1960s, when a very well known Asian art collector purchased the piece from a reputable New York dealer. The bronze was in his collection for a short time, and then he gave it to a friend and colleague, who kept it in her apartment for more than 30 years before a prominent dealer finally talked her into selling it to the Brooklyn Museum.'[3]

So continues the series on a kind of guide on collecting ethics and due diligence, but then it highlights the opaqueness of the system – while praising the museums' strict acquisitions policy, vital information is withheld for anonymity. We will see this repeated all through this book. It is a disease that plagues the art market. One of the easiest ways to escape public scrutiny is to withhold this kind of information. All the public is told is: we've done our due diligence, don't worry. But we cannot tell you anything more. No names or details will be divulged. You'll just have to trust us.

But this innocuous post led to a very innocuous comment in the comments thread underneath it. The person behind the comment ultimately led to the downfall of Kapoor's illicit empire. It was posted in April 2009, under the name Grace Paramaspry.

'Does this Siva has [sic] any history of passing through Mr. Subhash Kapoor in New York, (is) any part of the provenance history from UK?'

Cummins responded: 'We know the Shiva's history since the late 1960s, and in that time it was not in the UK, nor did it come through Subhash Kapoor.' Paramaspry now posted a message along the same lines on another blog entry authored by Cummins a couple of years ago.

Who was this Grace Paramaspry and what was the reason for this comment?

Despite all the flowery language in the post, why didn't the Brooklyn Museum answer the question? All they had to do was reveal the provenance paperwork for this acquisition. But they did not and continue to stonewall any questions to this day.

As for Grace Paramaspry, we need to head to Singapore.

A rather rundown shopping mall by Singapore's high standards, Tanglin Shopping Centre on Tanglin Road, just off the high-end Orchard Road, holds within it a sprinkling of 'art galleries' selling a myriad art pieces, from modern Buddha faces in eclectic colours to Khmer funeral reliquary. They hardly seem to have any visitors except for the occasional 'foreign' tourist looking for a cheap memento. But art galleries the world over are similar – they display a fraction of their actual stock, leaving the 'better' ones safe in their godowns for private viewings of their elite clients.

One such gallery at the Tanglin Shopping Mall was Jazmin Asian Arts, run by Grace Paramaspry Punusamy. Punusamy, who'd grown up in the island city-state, was the daughter of a Tamil father and a Chinese mother. She used to sell Kapoor's artefacts on consignment basis, and they began dating soon after they met in 1997.

As has been mentioned, Kapoor had married Neeru in 1976 in India, shortly before the family emigrated to America. The couple had a daughter, Mamta Kapoor, but they had divorced in 1986 and had been living separately since then. Very scant details are available about the

Grace–Subhash relationship, but they seem to have been quite a pair, embarking on many 'business development' trips into South-East Asia and creating a network of dealers and suppliers.

In fact, Kapoor was so comfortable with Grace that he started using her as cover for provenance paperwork which enabled him to create fake ownership records and helped to sell to prestigious museums – paperwork actually signed by Grace for his artefacts.

But sometime in 2008, after nearly a decade together, Kapoor ended their relationship. During this time Kapoor had started a relationship with another woman, Selina Mohamed, in America but it is not known if this was the reason for the split. What we do know is that Selina was also involved in Subhash's work. However, the parting was not peaceful, to say the least. They went to court in 2010 in Singapore to settle their business dealings. Kapoor won the case, displaying his shrewd business acumen and his relationship with dealers. This is what the *Straits Times* had to say in March 2010:

A Singaporean art dealer, who was in a relationship with an American art dealer, kept antiques worth hundreds of thousands of dollars after their affair soured two years ago. In an attempt to get these back, Mr. Subhash Kapoor, 61, took her to the High Court and succeeded. Delivering his verdict on Thursday, Judicial Commissioner Steven Chong said he agreed with Ms. Paramaspry Punusamy's lawyer that the case should have never come to court as it really was about a break-up between two lovers. The judge also noted that while both parties were unable to produce much in documentation to prove ownership of the 19 contested antiques, Mr Kapoor, 61, had called on three art traders from Bangkok to testify that they have sold some of the pieces to him. Ms Paramaspry, 54, did not produce any witnesses during the three-day hearing heard last month. Ms Punusamy, the proprietor of Jazmin Asian Arts at Tanglin Shopping Centre, was also ordered to pay costs for the proceedings.[3]

It is interesting to note a key finding by the judge that 'both parties were unable to produce much in documentation to prove ownership of the 19 contested antiques'.

Though this was not front-page news in conservative Singapore, the ACM, which had done business with Subhash Kapoor's Art of the Past, would have surely followed this case keenly.

Grace took the verdict badly. She had lost her case, money, artefacts and had also been publicly shamed. She was itching for retribution, hence her indiscreet and innuendo-laden comments on the Brooklyn Museum's website that had caught the attention of Indy and his team. Grace would in due course reach out to Indian law enforcement agencies to nail Subhash Kapoor and extract her sweet revenge.

We turn again to an extract from the confession of Subhash Kapoor to piece together the story in his own words:

> *My wife and I divorced in the year 1986–1987 in America and my wife is living separately now. My daughter Mamtha is presently 32 years old and she is living with her husband in New York . . .*
>
> *I could remember that the Chandrasekar bronze idol received from Sanjivi Ashokan was sold to a antique collector and now I believe it is in Brooklyn Museum . . .*
>
> *I created false provenance documents for all these stolen idols received from Sanjivi Ashokan with the help of my long time girlfriend Selena Mohammed, my employee Aaron Friedman and Jennifer Moore . . .*

His confession also stated that he had been in a relationship with Selena for ten years and that 'she has the access for my office and residence'.

8

Pedestal Inscription and an Anonymous Tip

While Indy was working hard trying to gather evidence, Subhash was living comfortably in the US. The authorities in India were looking for a hook to net this glittering big fish. They needed irrefutable evidence to corroborate Sanjeevi and his gang's story of Subhash's involvement in the Sripuranthan and Suthamalli robberies. And then just such a hook was delivered to us. In 2010 I received an anonymous tip! It was a magical email from an unknown scholar. This tip marked my entry into the Subhash Kapoor case which I had been following from afar till then.

At that time social media was just catching up in India. My blog poetryinstone.in had been up and running for two years. Through the blog I was building a community of like-minded art lovers – friends who shared a passion and an interest in showcasing the best of Indian art. We created groups and ran themed weeks like Shiva Week, Seated Vishnu Week and so on. We planned and went on documentation tours. We took a couple of weeks' leave and went off the grid on trips, photo-documenting the wonders of India.

We shared our images freely, with no restrictions on use, no copyrights, no watermarks. Our logic was, 'When the original creators, the sculptors, chose not to sign their works, choosing to remain anonymous, who were we to put our marks on these poor photographic renditions, captured with a click (though using expensive camera gear, after a day of surviving only on Maaza in a boondocks place, not even existing on maps)?'

Our aim was to build the largest e-archive of Indian art – whether in situ in India or at an auction house or gallery abroad. Social media helped us reach out to more people. International scholars, students and intrepid travellers submitted photos and helped us identify sculptures.

We encouraged more and more people to send us photos of Indian art that they encountered. Many such photographic submissions from around the world poured in. Our only request was to take one photo of the sender with the artefact, be it in a temple, museum, gallery or auction, and take one without any person. Thanks to India's IT boom which sent out trigger-happy techies to all corners of the world, we built the largest database of Indian art dispersed outside India.

Meanwhile, we also worked on fortifying our knowledge – buying, borrowing, scanning and discussing any book on Indian art. Friends and their families helped to scan the works for us, meticulously documenting every page, every photograph as we built our e-archive of Indian art.

We had diverse interests in the group – stone sculpture, cave temples, paintings, metal images and so on. I was particularly drawn to Chola processional bronzes. There were very few experts whom I trusted who had seen and studied them and very little documentation was available from bona fide sources. I wanted to become an expert on bronzes. At every opportunity during our temple documentation trips, we sought out processional deities, trying to understand their iconography, style and how they could be dated, for metal and stone images are impossible to scientifically date as they have no carbon content. Without carbon dating, expert opinion was divided and no two concurred on a date.

But the overwhelming feeling we got during our documentation and study was that everyone was suspicious of us. Experts would suddenly refuse to talk to us, temple authorities would literally throw us out for photographing the bronzes. Something was obviously amiss.

But the power of our community was in our numbers and enthusiasm. This was proved by that email I got in early 2010. It said that a gallery in America, Subhash Kapoor's Art of the Past, was putting up an inscribed matched pair of Shiva Nataraja and Sivakami for sale in Manhattan. As mentioned earlier, inscribed Chola bronzes are very rare and to find a hitherto undocumented one, that too a matched pair, was rarer than a blue moon. The photos sent to us showed that they were in impeccable condition. Their beauty stunned us but left us with a lingering suspicion. The coloration. They looked fresh from worship, for they even had residual oil stains. That must mean that they had only recently been removed from a temple in India – something that's not allowed. We worked on the photos to clear up the visibility of the inscription on the base pedestal. It read, 'Suthamalli' in the Tamil script.

We rushed to our temple database. We could find no temple by that name in Tamil Nadu. We looked up the gazette, inscriptions of India, South Indian inscriptions, volume after volume of PDF files. No luck. Suthamalli, as late as in 2010, was an unknown place even to us heritage hounds. While the robbery was discovered in 2008, neither that nor the Sripuranthan theft garnered enough media coverage, even though those raids are perhaps the most audacious to have ever taken place.

A dead end once again? It would be a terrible disappointment if it was.

There is a saying in Tamil that 'the many-day thief will get caught one day'. Even though these criminals had done meticulous checks, they did not know that there was a record of the idols they were looting. For that matter, even many in the scholarly world (thankfully) were not aware of this invaluable archive. A small research project in the calm, beachside, erstwhile French colony, now the Union Territory of Puducherry, held the clues – in a stack of ageing bin cards and microfilms.

The Institut Français de Pondichéry (IFP) had been

documenting temple sites in Tamil Nadu since 1955 and they had a good man at the helm – a research scholar and expert, Dr Murugesan.

The IFP archive team had visited the Sripuranthan temple as late as 23 November 1994 and Suthamalli on 24 June 1961 and photographed the bronzes while they were still in the temples. Their archive was not online and they had in place a complex system of bin cards and manual retrieval of photographic transparencies.

That's where we found archival photos of the two temples, Sripuranthan and Suthamalli. (A change of a single letter delayed our work quite a bit – the original inscription actually reads as 'Suthavalli' and that's what we had been searching for.) We soon found out that those two temples had been recently cleaned out by thieves.

Then there was another piece of evidence, also from early 2010, linking Subhash to the Suthamalli robberies. The *Arts of Asia* magazine's March 2010 issue contained

The IFP's archival photo of the Suthamalli Nataraja

a picture of Subhash Kapoor at Asia Week in New York, standing in front of a Nataraja and Sivakami. The caption read, 'Gallery owner Subhash Kapoor was proud of his rare and important bronze matched pair of the Shiva Nataraja and his consort Uma Paramesvari, Tamil Nadu, Chola Period, 12–13th century'. Kapoor was quoted as saying, 'It is quite amazing that the divine couple have not only survived as an original set, but also remain in complete state with their flaming prabhas and lotus pedestals.'[1]

They were the Suthamalli bronzes! The identification was complete. The proof was clear. It was time to link Subhash Kapoor to the thefts with foolproof evidence.

I immediately informed the Idol Wing and supplied them with the proofs – the email I had received and the photo of Subhash in the magazine. Selvaraj swung into action. It was around mid-2010 and our goal was within sight.

On a side point, if there is one piece of evidence needed to show how ill prepared the Indian authorities are for the fight that is on our hands it is a small incident that takes place around this time. The Idol Wing posted photos of the stolen sculptures, as received from the IFP, on their website as a PDF file. It was a sad reflection of their lack of technical and subject know-how – the images were in desperately poor resolution, had been badly resized and, above all, wrongly labelled – a Dancing Child Saint Sambandar was (and is still) labelled as Dancing Krishna, a standing saint Manickavasagar was (and is still) labelled as Sambandar. How can we expect to be taken seriously if even in a case of this prominence and significance the work done by our side is so shoddy?

We now return again to an extract from Subhash Kapoor's confession:

After seeing the photos, I offered to purchase all the bronze idols of Suthamally Temple and Sri Puranthan Temple since they belong to 11th-12th Century Chola Period . . .

As agreed upon by us, I received all the 8 [Sripuranthan] idols in 4 consignments before November 2006. It was sent from Everstar International Services owned by Packiakumar, partner of Sanjivi Ashokan, directly to my Nimbus Import Export Inc., New York . . . During March 2008, Sanjivi Ashokan contacted and informed about the despatch of shipment containing 10 antique bronze idols . . . taken away from Suthamally temple . . . I avoided direct shipment to New York fearing police and customs action as already impounded during February 2007. I directed my Hong Kong business contact Lai-sheung of Union Link Int. Movers (HK) Ltd., to re-divert these 10 idols to Neil Perry Smith at U.K. for restoration. Mr. Neil Perry Smith . . . cleaned the items and sent them to me at New York . . .

In one of the Nataraja bronze idols, I noticed some letter inscription made through engraving at the base of the idol. Through Sanjivi Asokan I understood it was 'Suthavalli' engraved in Tamil language meaning the name of the village. It is this village temple where from Sanjivi Ashokan and his associates took away the 18 Chola period bronze idols during 2008 . . . I have also sold some of these idols to various museums and private collectors.

9

Arrest in Germany

With Sanjeevi's naming of Subhash Kapoor and proof that he was in possession of the Suthamalli Nataraja and Sivakami, the tide was turning on Kapoor.

The police levelled a case of criminal conspiracy against Sanjeevi Asokan, Subhash Kapoor, and the other thieves. According to court documents, 'it was established that the petitioner [Subhash Kapoor] entered into a criminal conspiracy at Chennai and other places for committing theft of 18 Antique metallic idols from Sri Varadaraja Perumal Temple at Suthamalli village. A Non Bailable Warrant was issued [in July 2011] to the petitioner and for recovery of stolen idols . . . It was further found that the same gang was also involved in the theft of eight Antique metallic idols stolen from Sri Pragdeeswarar Temple at Sri Purandan village in Ariyalur District.'[1]

What was it alleged that they were criminally conspiring to do? Theft, forgery, house-breaking by night, cheating and receiving stolen property.

After this the wheels were set in motion to issue an Interpol red corner notice, that is, to seek the arrest of someone wanted in a particular jurisdiction in order to extradite them.

That's where Grace Paramaspry Punusamy, Subhash's bitter ex-girlfriend, steps in again. The previous year, in 2010, Subhash Kapoor had got into an online war of words with Damien Huffer, an American PhD scholar studying archaeology in Australia. Huffer had apparently been posting articles on his blog about how the finger of suspicion in various antique theft cases was pointing towards Subhash Kapoor. A livid Kapoor apparently wrote Huffer an email in early 2011 saying:

Dear Mr. Damien it has been brought to my attention you have been publishing unfounded truth rather Total lies spead [sic] by few people with no proof of fact or truth. I believe [sic] you have been miss guided [sic] and used by people who are trying to blackmail me . . . keep in mind you are not in the third world country and you can be held liable for the damages [sic] you are causing to my company and my name.

Huffer took down his posts but thereafter Kapoor trained his gun at who else but Grace Punusamy. On 22 February 2011, he wrote:

This woman in Singapore who have [sic] cheated many people and have changed her name many time [sic] over

the past many years typical of con artist [sic] i latest
hear that she change [sic] her company name again and
move [sic] to new shop.

   I assure you that i have not purchased any illegal
artworks from India and think of this in the past 4 years
i have traveled [sic] many countries including australia
if any interpol [sic] was informed i would have been
arrested by now. [2]

Clearly, Subhash Kapoor's spat with his ex-girlfriend
was still on the boil. Grace herself seems to have been
itching for revenge. A more dangerous kind of vengeance
than just griping over email. She approached the officers
of the Idol Wing, who were already on Kapoor's trail, and
gave them some valuable information. There is reason to
believe that the Indian authorities preferred not to have
to arrest Kapoor, a US citizen, in the States. Grace gave
them not just a recent photograph of Kapoor but also
tipped them off on his international movements. She
told the Idol Wing that Kapoor would be attending an
art fair in Germany in October 2011. That would be their
window to get him.

   'With the more recent photograph provided by
Punusamy and updates on Kapoor's location, it became
much easier to crack the case,' an investigating officer
said. On 30 October 2011, an unsuspecting Kapoor
walked up to an immigration counter at Frankfurt
International Airport. But instead of being stamped
through, Kapoor was taken into Interpol's custody. The

CBI had just five days before they were issued a red corner against Kapoor through Interpol. This was one of the rare times when India had issued an Interpol notice for antique theft.

Kapoor was in Interpol's custody for eight months – during which time Selvaraj retired – before he was extradited to India.

While Kapoor was in Interpol custody something very mysterious happened. He actually managed to smuggle out a handwritten note to his office. The note was written on the stationery of Wessing & Partner, a German law firm.

Below are some excerpts from the note dated 3 November 2011 addressed to Aaron Freedman, Subhash's assistant:

> *Dear Aaron,*
>   *I do not know how long I will be stuck here, so here are few things to take care.*
>   *Do not pay Sotheby's or Christies as they can wait!*
>   . . .
>   *Give back 4 items to Selina, Bronze dancers which are in the 4 closets.*

But there was a mysterious line in the note:

> *Talk to Shantoo and keep posted what he can do, tell him may be it is a time to make a deal.*[3]

What was the 'deal' that Subhash wanted his trusted associate Shantoo to make? Did it have anything to do with the Idol Wing mole?

WESSING & PARTNER

Nov 3rd 2011

DEAR AARON

FIRST OF ALL MY ~~HEIL ALBET~~ HEILKO AHLBRECHT MUST HAVE SPOKEN WITH YOU IF NOT HE CAN FILL YOU IN THE SITUATION I DONT KNOW HOW LONG I WILL BE STUCK HERE, SO HERE ARE FEW THINGS TO TAKE CARE

1 DO NOT USE THOSE CHECKS I LEFT WITH YOU AS YOU MIGHT NEED LATER. SO HERE NOW YOU WILL DO. FIRST EITHER OPEN NEW BANK ACCOUNT OR ASK SELINA TO DO. SHE CAN MAKE YOU AUTHORIZE TO SIGN THE CHECKS BETER IF YOU OPEN, WITH FIRST CHECK FOR 7000, DO NOT PAY SOTHEBY'S CHRISTIES AS THEY CAN WAIT

2. CALL VAZQUEZ AND BUY EURO TO SEND HEILKO THE ATTORNEY FOR RETAINER AMOUNT € 25000

3 LOOK LIKE JEU HAS TO DO WITH RUKMANI THE BEST SHE CAN, WE HAVE NO CHOICE.

4 KEEP GOOD TRACK OF THE MONEY IN THE ACCOUNT BY KEEPING GOOD RECORS OF DEPOSITS AS WELL AS WIRES, AND KEEP ME POSTED THROUGH MY HEILKO BEST SEND HIM EMAIL AND HE CAN PRINT OUT AND SHOW ME

5 TALK TO SHANTOO AND KEEP POSTED WHAT HE CAN DO, TEL HIM MAY BE IT IS A TIME TO MAKE A DEAL.

6 GIVE BACK 4 ITEMS TO SELINA BRONZE DANCERS WHICH ARE IN THE CLOSETS

7 ASK ANNE TO MAIL YOU MY KEYS IN THE BAG AND LET ME KNOW WHEN YOU GET THEM
ASK HER IF SHE CAN PICKUP MY BAG FROM AIRPORT SHE DONT HAVE RECEIPT SO SHE HAVE TO IDENTYFY THE BAG IT IS BLACK TRAVELPRO OR AMERCHA TEGRISTER IT HAVE TAG OF VIRGIN ATLANTIC WITH MY NAME IT HAVE A LOCK NO FOR THE LOCK 129, INSIDE HAVE 2 SUITS BLACK BLUE, 5-6 WHITE SHIRTS, PAIR OF BLACK SHOES, DUNHIL BELT SOME OTHER MISLANIOUS CLOTHS

Rathausufer 16-17
40213 Dusseldorf
Fon: +49(0)211 16844-0
Fax: +49(0)211 16844-444
Mail: societaet@justalrecht.de

Note from Subhash Kapoor to Aaron Freedman dated
3 November 2011

10

The Elusive Deendayal and the Hand-cut Nataraja

Sunday, 19 June 2005

Just as the sun was rising, Sundara Pattar, priest of the sixth-century Sri Narambunatha Swamy temple at Pazhuvur on the Tirunelveli–Kanyakumari border, administered by the HR&CEB, was walking towards the temple. He tucked the clunky keyring into his waist as he adjusted his dhoti. He expected a good weekend crowd even after taking into account that schools had already reopened. Little did he realize that the day would leave him permanently scarred.

When he reached the temple, he found the lock on the main door broken.

He wasted no time and raised an alarm. Immediately, the villagers assembled there. The police arrived an hour later. His worst nightmare had just played out in front of him – all thirteen of his bronze gods were gone, including his Nataraja and Sivakami.

A sniffer dog and fingerprint experts were pressed into service. The dog ran a few yards to the main road and lost the scent. The fingerprint experts took another two hours and went away. Then the police grilled him.

At first he couldn't believe that they could even think of suspecting him. He had cared for the idols as a son would – washed them, fed them, adorned them every single day for the past fifteen years, exactly how his father had taught him. His family had been living in service of the temple for generations – in fact, he knew of nothing outside the temple, his deity, his gods. Soon, the village folk also started casting glances at him. Did they also suspect him? He nodded in disbelief. Surely not!

He tried to think clearly and remember. Saturday, 18 June . . . Did he notice anything strange? Coming to think of it, yes. He had seen some new faces in the temple in the past few months. At first he hadn't taken note, but then the same group of people showed up again and again.

Yes, they were there on 18 June as well. He remembered they were in the temple till the last puja. He had just assumed they were devout pilgrims. He was about to mention this to the police when the temple's executive officer, K. Velusamy, came in.

His arrival gave Pattar some confidence and he wrote down his suspicions. Accordingly, a case was registered at the Pazhuvur police station. Did the executive officer have any photographs of the bronzes?[1]

No!

There was no follow-up by the authorities and finally, a year later, in 2006, the case was transferred to the Idol Wing, which narrowed down its list and identified a few men belonging to Madurai and surrounding areas as suspects.

According to the investigators, 'Shakti Mohan, a small-scale gold merchant, and his acquaintance Arumugam, a pickpocket, both from Madurai, stole the idols from the temple, believing them to be made of gold. But as they tried to get away, Arumugam's motorcycle met with an accident. So, with the help of Balaji, Shakti Mohan's son, and another man called Saudi Murugan, they hid the idols in a pond.'[2]

They also disfigured some idols, including the priceless and stunning Nataraja, cutting off the Lord's famed left hand, seeking gold. Disappointed at not finding any gold, they sold the remaining idols to one Dhinakaran, a merchant in Karaikudi. Since the damage done to the idols reduced their selling price, an argument arose and in the ensuing scuffle Shakti Mohan was killed.

But then the plot gets interesting. The Idol Wing traced the Nataraja idol to the major Chennai-based antique dealer Deendayal, an associate of Subhash Kapoor's, who purchased the idols from Dhinakaran. Five idols, including the Nataraja and a Manickavasagar, a ninth-century Tamil poet-saint who wrote one of the

Hand-cut Nataraja

key religious texts of the Shaivites, were apparently
sent through a handler, Vallabh Prakash (who was also
involved in the Australia Ardhanarishvara deal), to
Subhash Kapoor.[3]

After that the case went limp for five-odd years.
Meanwhile, Kapoor routed the Nataraja to an associate
in London, a world-renowned expert in art restoration,
who fashioned a new hand for the Nataraja and the idol

Hand-cut Nataraja after restoration

eventually found itself in New York, adorning the cover of Kapoor's Art of the Past catalogue in March 2007, with a price tag of $2.5 million!

On 8 August 2011, just months before the arrest of Subhash Kapoor, the hand-cut Nataraja made a low-key appearance back in Chennai, on the website of the Idol Wing of all places, apparently returned by a well-meaning Chennai dealer. The website reported this as an important recovery, a feather in the cap of the Idol Wing.

The dealer who returned five of the stolen idols was none other than Deendayal, but that information was withheld at that time. The case of the hand-cut Nataraja seemed to be alive again, right? Wrong.

Once the idols had been returned the heat magically cooled off all the suspects in this case (other than Subhash, of course). But what explains the five-year wait to make amends? With the ante being upped in the Subhash Kapoor case there must have been widespread panic in the 'art world' about who else would bite the dust. Better to pay your dues, atone and make nice with the cops was the word on the street. Give the cops a way out, a small victory so that in the din of celebration they could hide some sins.

As The Hindu reported an Idol Wing officer saying, 'After tightening of the noose, the smugglers decided to bring back the five idols, all worth Rs. 200 crore.'[4] But the bizarre thing is that the law enforcement machinery seemed to have acquiesced to this weird 'amnesty'. No arrests were made. It was as though all was forgotten, the cops and robbers seemed to have kissed and made up. How could a criminal justice system work this way? Thirteen idols were stolen, five returned, all was well? If this sounds disjointed, illogical and bizarre, dear reader, it's because it is.

That the accused could swing such a sweetheart deal seems stunning. Almost as though the accused had leverage over someone in the Idol Wing. Yes, of course, they must have. Could it have been because of the suspected mole in the department?

In early 2008, a French tourist couple were on a month-long journey of exploration in Tamil Nadu. They were spending the last week of their trip in the famed temple town of Madurai. They were visiting a studio in South Mada Street for purchasing memory cards for their Nikon camera, when they saw photos of two bronzes inside – Shiva and Parvati. Intrigued, they struck up a conversation with the owner, Sundaramoorthy, who straight away offered them the two bronzes for ₹3 crore each.

Sundaramoorthy explained to them that the bronze idols were from a buried hoard and hence were not stolen ones. He got them to talk to Santhanam, a resident of Aladipatty village in Virudunagar district, who informed them that the bronzes had been found a few months earlier when his friend, a 'farmer', Arokiaraj, was tilling his land. He had found more idols, and if they were interested he could show them four more. What they didn't know was that even buried idols legally belong to the government thanks to the Indian Treasure Trove Act of 1878. You cannot walk home with them!

Shocked, they rushed out of the shop and after a night of deliberation, decided to inform the local police station. The local police immediately called the Idol Wing in Chennai. The call went to Kader Batcha, Selvaraj's junior who led the Emerald Linga bust in order to see if it went according to plan. Batcha and an aide apparently promptly arrived at the studio pretending to be potential buyers, but Sundaramoorthy saw through their cover and claimed ignorance. At this point the investigation got rather rough and Constable N. Subburaj joined them. With guns drawn, the accused were taken to an undisclosed location. The police also caught Arokiaraj and after a couple of days of questioning, they seized all the six bronzes.

Once again, in what should have been an open-and-shut case, no formal arrests were made and the seizures were not recorded. So what happened to the idols? Sure enough, Batcha and company returned to Chennai with all six bronzes. But instead of handing them over to the relevant people in the Idol Wing, they secretly transported them to the godown of none other than Deendayal. There, a price was 'negotiated' for some of the idols. According to a petition filed in the Madras High Court, the Sivakami and a bronze sculpture depicting Lord Shiva and Goddess Parvati with their infant son Skanda (such idols are known as Somaskanda) were sold 'to Dinadayalan, a noted smuggler at Chennai for Rs. 15 Lakhs, which in turn, were sold allegedly for Rs 6 Crores'.[5]

The Somaskanda was then sold by Deendayal to Subhash Kapoor who supposedly sold it on to a prominent collector in Bangkok.

All six idols are yet to be retrieved.

But what happened to Kader Batcha? An FIR was subsequently registered naming him as an accused – Arokiaraj ratted him out.[6] But Batcha was still promoted within the organization and no departmental proceeding or arrest was made. When an enquiry was launched, the petition in the high court says, it was assigned to a subordinate officer of Batcha's in the same department! How could justice possibly be done?

Finally, the Madras High Court had to intervene and insist that, 'an order of suspension dated 29.06.2017 was passed'. By then Batcha had been on the run for a few months, since February 2017. He was finally only arrested in September that year and is now awaiting trial.[7] His request for first-class facilities in prison were denied by the court.[8]

So, Batcha, it would appear, had been hand in glove with Deendayal and others in the trade all along. This fact was confirmed by Subhash Kapoor. *The Hindu* reported, 'It was Khader Basha, Kapoor said, who regularly smuggled and sold idols from a number of temples. Apparently, the cop often did it under the guise of taking them to a central storage facility for "safekeeping from idol thieves"... the stolen original would be replaced by a sophisticated fake.'

The report continued, 'Additional clues, all confirmed by intelligence sources, suggest that Basha was deeply involved in the network of idol smugglers. One such indicator was the fact that despite pressure from other agencies, the police team led by Basha was initially unwilling to raid the Indo-Nepal Gallery in Mumbai. It was suspected that stolen idols held by two antique dealers, Vallabh Prakash and his son Aditya Prakash, were stored at this gallery.'[9]

Vallabh is the man who helped Subhash Kapoor get that Ardhanarishvara statue that was ultimately sold to the AGNSW. This shows us how Batcha helped his crony associates by going easy on them.

Could Batcha's compromised position explain the gentle treatment meted out to Deendayal in the hand-cut Nataraja case? Did Batcha only execute the Emerald Linga bust perfectly because he was worried that he would be found out if the operation failed? And do these facts help explain Subhash Kapoor's note and the 'deal' he alluded to? When he smuggled it out while in custody in Germany in 2011, we didn't know what the note meant. Now it seems we may have an explanation.

In a subsequent note to Aaron Freedman, his assistant and gallery manager, Subhash wrote: *'Call Shantoo and ask him to call Valab and tell him "Kader Batcha want me to come India. If I come I will tell every thing, every detail of every thing, so if you don't want me to tell make suar* [sure] *he don't force me." Tell Valab exactly like this.'*[10]

Was Subhash Kapoor attempting to blackmail an

CALL SHANTOO AND ASK HIM TO CALL VALAB AND TELL HIM "KADER BADCHA WANT ME TO COME INDIA. IF I COME I WILL TELL EVERY THING, EVERY DETAIL OF EVERY THING, SO IF YOU DONT WANT ME TO TELL MAKE SUAE HE DONT FORCE ME."
TELL VALAB EXACTLY LIKE THIS

KEEP SENDING ME THE DETAILS OF PROGRESS AND DAILY WORK SO I CAN GIVE FUATHER INSTRUCTIONS

Second note from Subhash Kapoor to Aaron Freedman

officer of the Idol Wing in a last-ditch attempt to save his own skin? How deep was the rot in the system?

Even if Subhash Kapoor was trying to blackmail someone, threatening to spill some beans on them, his case was far too advanced and high profile to be thwarted now. The Ministry of External Affairs, along with the Idol Wing, set in motion the process to extradite Subhash.

Undeterred, Kapoor filed an audacious case in the Madras High Court while he was locked up in Germany through his sister, Sushma Rani Sareen, to whom he had given power of attorney. The case challenged the legality of the non-bailable arrest warrant issued by the Indian authorities that would lead to his extradition. His arguments? In brief that 'The attempt to extradite the petitioner [Subhash Kapoor] based upon the confession statement of the co-accused [Sanjeevi Asokan] was bad.'

The judge's response: 'The contention raised that the confession of the co-accused cannot be relied cannot be accepted. The confession of the co-accused if it implicated him, it is also admissible in evidence.' Kapoor's petition was dismissed.[11]

But he didn't give up – his lawyers went to the Supreme Court in June 2012. But the apex court, too, refused to quash the non-bailable warrant. The court told Kapoor: 'You are a north Indian while all other accused are from the south. Why would they take your name during the questioning by police? The business you have in New York has some nexus with the case. In this situation, we cannot grant any relief.'[12]

It seemed that Subhash Kapoor would at last face justice in India.

Finally, on 14 July 2012, a team of Idol Wing police officers landed at Chennai airport, along with Kapoor. Clad in black trousers and blue shirt, Kapoor smiled at the reporters waiting there as he was escorted out by the police team to prison.

But his old friend Sanjeevi Asokan wasn't there to give him company. Early on, in an unbelievable twist to the story, despite Selvaraj's best efforts, and the incriminating evidences against the well-connected Sanjeevi, he was granted bail. In March 2018, Sanjeevi would again be arrested, for another set of suspected crimes. He is still under trial and the cases against him have not been decided.

These days Kapoor spends his days with the other inmates in a prison in Chennai while his trials continue apace. But for a man who was once the toast of the New York cocktail circuit, gone are the fine bespoke suits and silk ties. Subhash can be spotted with tousled hair and a days-old stubble in the prison yard wearing a blue T-shirt and brown shorts. Apparently, he has been exempted from wearing the regulation white prison uniform. A small favour for the big fish. As *The Hindu* noted in 2017, 'The 69-year-old Subhash Kapoor doesn't look the part of a man said to be the kingpin of an international gang of idol thieves.'[13]

How the mighty fall.

11

The Ardhanarishvara and the Nataraja

In the months and years after his arrest, antiquities associated with Subhash Kapoor would reveal themselves on every continent of the globe. The skeletons that came tumbling out of the closet will be hugely helpful in securing a conviction, as Kapoor is still under trial. Especially because, unlike in the past, we have been able to secure the repatriation of an unprecedented number of idols. While we've been trying our hardest to bring home our gods, museums around the world have been stonewalling our efforts. They would rather keep them in their glass cages. And they certainly don't want to come clean on their association with Kapoor and how they went on an unethical buying spree that ensured their cash kept his coffers full.

It was the morning of 28 June 2013. Call it destiny, fate or serendipity – the first thing I saw upon waking up was an article in *The Hindu*, 'New Images of Stolen Nataraja Surface' by A. Srivathsan.

Following Kapoor's extradition to India, in January 2013 the Indian authorities sent letters rogatory to Australia asking for information after making a visual match between the Sripuranthan Nataraja, which had been stolen in 2006, and a Nataraja acquired by the NGA in 2008. A letter rogatory is just a legal term for making a request of information through a foreign court to a person or entity (in this case the NGA) within the jurisdiction of that court.

But the Aussies denied having even received the letter! According to *The Hindu*, 'The NGA denied receiving it. When *The Hindu* got in touch with the Australian Attorney General's Department that handles international requests for assistance, it refused to either confirm or deny the receipt of a letter rogatory.'[1]

Thanks to an active online community of bloggers, newspapers and true art lovers, the pressure was maintained on the NGA. But the museum repeatedly stonewalled demands that they declare their transactions history with Kapoor and the ownership histories of the pieces they had purchased. The gallery's director even said during a hearing of the Australian Senate that they would not divulge any information as he was confident that none of the Kapoor objects had been looted.[2] But it was clear to everyone that the NGA had been buying from Subhash Kapoor without verifying the provenance of antiquities properly.

Finally when the NGA did come out and speak they

THE ART LOSS ■ REGISTER™
                                              www.artloss.com

LONDON - NEW YORK - COLOGNE - AMSTERDAM

April 20th 2007

Art of the Past, Inc.
1242 Madison Avenue
New York, NY 10128

ALR Ref: AOP 260-4

Dear Mr.

We have now carried out a search of the Art Loss Register's database for the following item:

ITEM:	Shiva Nataraja
CIVILIZATION:	Tamil Nadu
DATE/PERIOD:	11th-12th century, chola period
COUNTRY OF ORIGIN:	South India
MEDIUM:	Bronze
DIMENSIONS:	52 inches
PROVENANCE PROVIDED:	Not provided

We certify that this item has not, to the best of our knowledge, been registered as stolen or missing on our database of stolen and missing art nor has a claimant reported this work to us as a loss between 1933 and 1945. It should, however, be noted that:

• not every loss or theft is reported to us
• the database does not contain information on illegally exported artifacts unless they have been reported to us as stolen
• the ALR does not have details of all works of art confiscated, looted or subjected to a forced seizure or forced sale between 1933 and 1945.

It is also important for you to note that this Certificate is no indication of authenticity of the item.

We do not guarantee the provenance of any item against which we have made a search. Your search with The Art Loss Register demonstrates due diligence but may not excuse you undertaking further research or providing further information where known. Should we become aware of any abuse of this Certificate we may find it necessary take action.

If we can be of service to you again, please do not hesitate to contact us.

Yours sincerely,

Katherine M. Dugdale
THE ART LOSS REGISTER

Art Loss Register certificate for the Sripuranthan Nataraja

released a statement accepting the fact that they had bought twenty-two items from Subhash Kapoor. But the details were sketchy. Regarding the Nataraja, the museum went to great lengths to explain how they engaged in due diligence for a year, went to the US to see the Nataraja, consulted the ALR, where the Nataraja was not listed, looked up the websites of the Tamil Nadu Police and even consulted an unnamed (but of course) 'expert' on Chola art and an unnamed (again) ASI official. The irrepressible *Hindu* noted, 'This correspondent spoke to some well-known experts in ancient sculptures in Chennai; all of them denied any knowledge of the Nataraja. The NGA had not contacted them. Police sources confirmed they were not contacted either. They pointed out that the letter issued by the ALR does not establish that the Nataraja was not a stolen one. All it states is that the artefact is not in the register . . . Another claim by the NGA that it had checked records of the ASI before purchasing the Nataraja is not verifiable since the gallery does not provide names of the persons it consulted.'

But that's just the background. On the morning of 28 June 2013, *The Hindu* reported what my colleagues, the unstoppable Jason Felch and Ralph Frammolino, had published on chasingaphrodite.com: 'The most damaging evidence challenging the claims of the NGA'. The NGA had been saying that they had a document to prove that Kapoor bought the Nataraja from a man in Washington, DC in 2004. But Jason and Ralph published two pictures from 2006 on their blog that showed the Sripuranthan Nataraja in India shortly after it had been stolen from the temple. These were pictures that had been emailed to Subhash Kapoor in 2006. How could the NGA's document be legit if the Nataraja was in India in 2006? Where did the question arise of Kapoor buying the

Nataraja from a man in DC in 2004 if the Nataraja was still in India?

'The story of the Washington owner was a fabrication, the records show.'[3]

But the NGA shockingly dug its heels in and refused to admit that theirs was the Sripuranthan Nataraja. After all they had paid a whopping $5 million for it!'

After reading the news I immediately went to Jason's website. The robber photos of the Sripuranthan Nataraja in the NGA were startling. Yes, they were clearly the robber photos, showing the stunning and enormous Nataraja in a safe house in India.

But while there was a wall of resistance from the NGA, another Australian museum was behaving differently. A post on Jason's blog caught my eye: 'Coming Clean: Australia's Art Gallery of New South Wales Releases Kapoor Documents'.

Alongside the NGA, we had been applying pressure on the Sydney-based AGNSW to reveal its transactions history with Subhash Kapoor. They finally put this out. They had been acquiring stuff from Kapoor between 1994 and 2004. But not just that, they put out the ownership history of one of the objects acquired from Kapoor.

The AGNSW was an exception in its openness because of its new director, Michael Brand. In 2005, he had been appointed director of the Getty Museum, struggling with the Italian allegations of acquiring stolen artefacts. Brand instituted a regime of transparency at the Getty, established rigorous new requirements for checking the

Robber photos of the Sripuranthan Nataraja

provenance of future acquisitions and made peace with Italy and Greece through agreements on restitution and reciprocal loans. Somehow, he steered the Getty out of the storm. At the AGNSW, he would, in time, put all the Kapoor purchases, with supporting provenance paperwork, in the public domain. Not that there was much paperwork. Even superficial, 'optical' due diligence, to borrow a term Jason coined, was absent in the purchases made in the 1990s.

A complete list of clients and associates of Kapoor is given in Appendix 3. This list has been taken from the Internet from the archived pages of Art of the Past. None of these museums, galleries or private collectors, except the AGNSW, volunteered to disclose details about their purchases from the arrested dealer even after two years of the Interpol notice. So much for transparency and ethics in the art market.

But coming back to the ownership history of that first object the AGNSW put out.

The salient points were summarized in Jason's post:

Ardhanarishvara

In 2004, the Gallery purchased this Chola-period sculpture from Kapoor for more than [US] $300,000 . . . The image of Ardhanarishvara was likely in a niche on an external wall.

Kapoor provided two documents with the sculpture.

One is a receipt dated 1970, purportedly from Uttam Singh and Sons, the Delhi 'copper and brass palace' [that's how the establishment describes itself on the

Uttam Singh & Sons

COPPER & BRASS PALACE
INDIAN ARTS, HANDICRAFTS DEALERS & EXPORTERS

Show Room :
1038, PAIWALAN,
NEAR JAMA MASJID
DELHI-110006

Office :
1038, CHAWRI BAZAR
NEAR JAMA MASJID
DELHI-110006

Phone OH. : 24 53 90
Res. : 39 32 87

Ref. No. 70/357

Date 15/4/1970

To,
Abdulla Mehgoub
D 220 Deffence Colony
New Delhi

Standing Aradhnareshwara with Nandi
Granite Stone South India
Chola Period 12th C. Height 4 Ft.

Rs. 25,000.00

Indian Rupee Twenty Five Thousand.

Receipt from Uttam Singh and Sons

Art Of The Past

1242 Madison Avenue New York, NY 10128, Phone (212) 860-7070, Fax (212) 876-5171

LETTER OF PROVENANCE
March 25th 2003

I, Raj Mehgoob, hereby certify that the Granite sculpture of Aradhanareshwara leaning
over the nandi from South India, Tamil Nadu, Chola, 10th Century, Dimensions: 46 ½ x
19 x 12 inches was purchased by my husband, Abdulla Mehgoub who was diplomat in
Delhi from Sudan during his posting there from 1968 to 1971

Raj Mehgoub
63-58 grand Central Parkway

Letter of provenance for the Vriddhachalam Ardhanarishvara
from Raj Mehgoub

receipt] that sold the sculpture to a private collector [Abdulla Mehgoub].

The second document purports to be a 2003 'Letter of Provenance' on letterhead from Art of the Past, Kapoor's Madison Ave. gallery. It is signed by 'Raj Mehgoub', who claims to be the wife of a diplomat who lived in Delhi from 1968 to 1971.[4]

Institut Français de Pondichéry / École française d'Extrême-Orient

Vriddhachalam Ardhanarishvara

But all my attention was on a picture of the Ardhanarishvara. I felt a trickle of cold sweat.

It was my favourite Vriddhachalam Ardhanarishvara! The same one I had referred to in my blogpost many years ago, without realizing that the robbers had already stolen it from its niche. The temple it's from (Vriddhagisvarar temple in Vriddhachalam) is a stone's throw from my village. I rushed to my notes and looked for published references. There was no doubt that the AGNSW's sculpture was indeed the Vriddhachalam Ardhanarishvara. Two of the main hands were broken in exactly the same way and place.

I shot out emails to *The Hindu*'s Srivathsan and Michaela Boland of the *Australian*.

I told them that I had just managed to trace the origin and history of the Ardhanarishvara mentioned by the AGNSW. I attached a picture from Douglas Barrett's book *Early Cola Architecture and Sculpture* published in 1974 – when the kosta, or niche, sculpture was intact in the Vriddhachalam temple.

Things began to fall in place pretty quickly after that. I posted on Facebook: 'Anyone from Vriddhachalam? Need urgent help – should be able to visit the temple immediately.'

Within an hour one of my best friends and part of the poetryinstone team, Satheesh, arranged to send his friend to the temple. But we found that there was still an Ardhanarishvara sculpture in the relevant niche in the temple. Quickly, we were able to determine that the kosta Ardhanarishvara idol present in the temple was not the original one, but a copy! How did we know that? The clue was in the lower right hand. Iconography stipulates that the hand lay flat on the head of the bull. But the sculptor who made the copy was most certainly a novice who did not know the agamas well. He has sculpted the lower right hand in abhaya hasta (that symbolizes the bestowing of protection). My heart sank and I was full of rage. What kind of a person does such a thing to a temple?

I wrote an email to Michaela about why I considered the idol in Australia to be the original and also gave references to works (one book published in 1974 and another in 1983) that proved that the original idol was in the temple till 1973–74. Why is this important? Because as mentioned earlier, 1972 is the cut-off date after which the recipient country of an object older than 100 years taken out of India will have to forfeit it without compensation. As long as we are able to show that the sculpture was in India till around 1972, the Australians would have to return it, no questions asked, no compensation paid.

Meanwhile, Srivathsan proceeded to check out the shop in Delhi, Uttam Singh and Sons, from where the sculpture was supposedly bought, and came back with this:

> I spoke to one of Uttam Singh's sons – the owner of the handicrafts shop in Delhi.
>
> Uttam Singh is no more, and his son cannot recollect selling any Nataraja or stone sculptures in the 1970s. When I explained to him about the receipt and the context of the enquiry, he denied that his father or shop would have sold stolen objects.

Uttam Singh used to sign in Urdu and not English, his son emphasized. Jason, can you verify whether the receipt was signed in Urdu or English?

The receipt was in fact typed in English but was not signed at all.

The weekend *Australian* carried our findings as full-page news, turning the screws further on the AGNSW. It caustically said:

It takes about seven minutes to walk from the Art Gallery of NSW, across the Domain in Sydney to the gallery's sister institution, the State Library of NSW.

Had curators at the gallery made that walk in 2004, before they finalized the [US]$300,000 acquisition of a magnificent 1000-year-old rock carving of Ardhanarishvara...they might have become suspicious that the carving had been stolen.

In the library's reference section there's a copy of Douglas E. Barrett's 1974 book *Early Cola Architecture and Sculpture*, 866–1014 AD. The library's copy is one of 21 copies of the revered archaeologist's landmark publication that can be found in public institutions across the nation.

Among a limited number of pictures in the book of Chola era carvings photographed at Indian temples is No. 54, a stone Ardhanarishvara with Nandi in Vriddhachalam in the southern Indian state of Tamil Nadu, which bears an uncanny resemblance to AGNSW's Ardhanarishvara.

Based on this photograph, University of Sydney art theft scholar Damien Huffer says he's confident the statue in the Sydney gallery's collection was lifted off the wall of an Indian temple. Going by the publication date of Barrett's book, this is likely to have happened some time after 1973 or 1974 – which means it was, by definition, removed illegally from India . . .

Huffer says the gallery's curators undertook insufficient due diligence before the purchase.

'For a museum or gallery to truly perform due diligence requires that they bring all of their often considerable resources to bear to assess all available published information, and not merely what the dealer suggests,' he says.[5]

We would later see that even the IFP had photographed the statue in 1974 – another piece of proof that the sculpture was in India well after the cut-off year of 1972.

The Hindu's follow-up story was equally important, because it turned the screws on the incompetent Indian authorities.

The authorities in Vriddhagisvarar temple seemed blissfully unaware of the lost sculpture and insisted that Ardhanarisvara was still there, pointing to the idol which is in worship. But this idol has no resemblance to the one photographed by Barrett and IFP. The authorities claimed that there were no records of either theft or replacement of the sculpture.[6]

Two months later the Indian Police finally confirmed that the idol in the AGNSW was indeed stolen from the temple. In 2002, the temple officials themselves removed the Ardhanarishvara (along with seven other sculptures!) as it was 'partly damaged'. The officials themselves put in its place a poor replica! The original, a priceless piece of Chola heritage, was thankfully kept inside the temple complex. But think about what this means: a theft that had to have occurred between 2002 (the date the original was replaced with a replica) and 2004 (when the AGNSW acquired the original) was only discovered in 2013 when I, a shipping executive in Singapore, happened to raise a stink!

The joint commissioner of the HR&CEB registered a complaint with the police in July 2013 regarding the theft of the Ardhanarishvara sculpture from the Vriddhagisvarar temple.

Sadly, despite all the focus, my colleagues and I had not done a thorough job on the same temple and after two years we realized our folly. As mentioned earlier, Kapoor had sold the Ardhanarishvara to the AGNSW in 2004 for $300,000 and a Sharabanimurthi to the NGA for AUS$328,244 on 1 June 2005. That sculpture, too, was from the same temple.

The ICE authorities 'were able to identify the smugglers of the Ardhanari to be the Prakashs, a family that owns and operates Indo-Nepal Art Centre, a gallery in Mumbai. In 2002, the Prakashs [Vallabh and Aditya] offered the stolen Ardhanari to Kapoor at Art of the Past and he purchased it and together they had it smuggled to the United States [via Hong Kong]. Kapoor proceeded to sell the idol with false paperwork to the Art Gallery of New South Wales in 2004 . . . Dean Dayal appears to have been the mastermind on the ground behind the actual thefts at the temples, while the Prakashs appear to have been the "brokers" or the individuals who would sell the stolen idols wholesale and then smuggle them out of India.'[7] Vallabh Prakash's name has come up a few times before in this book: not just in the context of the Ardhanarishvara sculpture but also in the hand-cut Nataraja case, in Subhash's letter to Aaron asking him to cut a 'deal' with the Indian authorities, and it was his gallery that *The Hindu* reported Kader Batcha was reluctant to raid at one point.

Interestingly, in December 2013 I visited the IFP for getting some information for a different case, when my visit was interrupted by a plain-clothes policeman. He said he was working for the Idol Wing in Chennai and had been sent by the Deputy Inspector General of Police (DIG), Pon Manikkavel, with a written request for the front and back photographs of the stolen Vriddhachalam Ardhanarishvara statue. Dr Murugesan, the director, gently explained to him that these were niche sculptures and thus he had only the photographs of the front.

I was at another desk and looking at the bin cards. Dr Murugesan gave him the required picture. When the policeman saw it, he asked, 'What is this half-man, half-lady statue?' It left the poor researcher stumped. But what came next stumped me as well.

'Sir, some jobless idiot in Singapore has given some

information to *The Hindu* and I had to come all the way from Chennai to Pondicherry to get this photo for the case file.'

Dr Murugesan thankfully hid his smile and advised him that, in future, all the Idol Wing had to do was to send an official email request and the IFP would send the photos via email attachments.

After the policeman left, this jobless idiot went about the task of cracking a few more cases.

The Ardhanarishvara case was the tipping point in the Subhash Kapoor investigation, as it was the first time we could use the UN Convention: we could prove that, one, the theft had happened in 2002, two, the provenance paperwork for the Uttam Singh receipt was forged, and, three, the provenance paperwork citing Sudanese diplomat Abdulla Mehgoub and Raj Mehgoub was fake. The Australians would have to return our God.

From the temple in Tamil Nadu to the AGNSW in Australia – the statue had taken less than two years to make the transition from a sacred deity to a museum showpiece. Kapoor had made the cardinal error in illicit trafficking by not fencing the idol for a while before bringing it out. Fencing means disguising the stolen nature of an object by keeping it hidden from the public eye until the search for it becomes a vague memory, and also by adding middlemen in the journey of the object from the thieves to the final buyer. This mistake forced the Australian authorities to reveal every record of their purchases, not only from Kapoor but for every Indian artefact purchased in the last forty years, revealing many more such dubious purchases.

The work of the IFP has to be lauded, not just for academic contribution, but also for documenting our heritage treasures for law enforcement reasons. My work with the IFP started off casually, when I almost pleaded with them for access to their archives. Later, it blossomed into a great partnership.

Like the rest of the 'premier' art institutions of the world, the NGA, too, was refusing to divulge any significant information about its purchases from Subhash Kapoor and Art of the Past. The face of the NGA at that time was its director, Ron Radford.

Radford had replaced Brian Kennedy at the top post at the NGA in 2004 and much of the problematic dealings with Kapoor happened after that, though the NGA had been buying from Kapoor since before 2004.

At the peak of the scandal, according to a report, Kennedy, who took over as director of the Toledo Museum of Art in Ohio, USA, said he didn't know that the NGA was buying from Kapoor during his tenure. In a telling story about the way in which Kapoor functioned, Kennedy even revealed that he once walked away from a dodgy purchase because Kapoor didn't put the piece on show at his gallery, Art of the Past. 'He took me to an apartment to show me a work of art and I thought it was rather strange,' claims Kennedy. He further states that Kapoor couldn't tell him its provenance. But for all Kennedy's protestations, the NGA had been buying from Kapoor during his term as director. In fact starting 2002, a series of problematic transactions with Kapoor are on record.[8]

Meanwhile, Michaela was working with Jason and together they were putting out information about the Sripuranthan Nataraja that was increasingly exposing and troubling the NGA.

But it seemed the NGA was hard to shame. Even after Jason published robber photos of the Sripuranthan Nataraja, they continued to deny that it was the piece they had. The museum put out the following statement:

'The National Gallery of Australia believes there is yet to emerge any conclusive evidence to demonstrate that the 11th–12th century bronze sculpture of Shiva as Lord of the Dance [Shiva Nataraja] in its collection was stolen or illegally exported from India. The Gallery notes that criminal proceedings against Art of the Past dealer Subhash Kapoor are ongoing.'[9]

When the NGA's director was taken to the Idol Wing website with the photographs of the missing idols, he dismissively said:

They posted very bad photographs that didn't look like the same one. The dancing Shiva is an iconic style and

small, bad photographs do not reveal it. I have to say it
didn't look like the same work. Some journalists have
jumped to that conclusion, but we in an art museum
don't.[10]

The media lit into the gallery. But instead of throwing
open its doors the gallery constituted an enquiry
committee headed by Radford, under whose tenure the
Sripuranthan Nataraja was purchased in the first place,
and a senior curator of Asian art. Could there be any
more glaring a conflict of interest?

Even though the NGA itself decided to sue Subhash
Kapoor for 'fraud' and 'breach of contract . . . based on
fraudulent sale of an antiquity', Radford was on record
saying the NGA would not return the Nataraja to India
unless further evidence of wrongdoing was furnished![11]
Talk about hypocrisy.

There was no doubt after examining the high
resolution photographs of the Sripuranthan Nataraja
from the IFP that it was the same one as the Nataraja
now in the NGA. An in-depth analysis revealed
multiple matches, including small cuts and breakages
in the idol.

At this point Radford could do little. The pressure
on the Australian government was enormous. As the
return of the Sripuranthan Nataraja seemed imminent,
on 2 May 2014, Subhash Kapoor panicked and on 7
May 2014, while still in jail in Tamil Nadu, he sent a
note through his lawyer Kingston Jerold, which he then

arranged to be mailed to senator and attorney general of Australia, George Brandis, with a copy to Radford. The letter is reproduced here:

Dear Mr. Attorney General,

In the past few weeks I have come to know through newspapers that the DANCING SHIVA NATARAJA you are planning to return to Government of India. It is your property now and you have all the right to do as you please, but if you planning to give to Government of India claiming it is stolen then I must bring to your attention that this dancing shiva is not stolen.

The Government of India have not proven it in the court as of this date that this dancing shiva Nataraja is stolen.

I am confident that they can never be able to prove it is stolen and that is the reason even after promises to the Government of Germany for speedy trail [trial], Government of India have not even begun the trial or even given me the chargesheet as of this day after almost 2 years.

Government of India does not have any proof that this Dancing Shiva is stolen and that is the reason they have not proceeded in the Court but continue to proceed in the Media.

On the one hand they have restricted me as the extent that I do not have privacy of attorney client and not been permit me to contact my family or my attorney in New York. On the other hand they are fabricating the story as they go along to prove me guilty only in the media.

Police know very well that this Dancing Shiva is

not stolen and have demanded SIX CRORES OF RUPEE (APPROXIMATELY ONE MILLION US DOLLARS) to close the case.

I have refused to pay them as a principle. I do not wish to give any BRIBE OR SUBMIT MY SELF TO ANY EXTORTION.

I am confident that I can prove my innocence and this dancing Shiva is not stolen in the Court of Law. I suggest you to be patient and not be in hasty to give this Dancing Shiva to the Government of India until the trial is finished.

Sincerely

Subhash Kapoor

It would be critical now to keep up the pressure on the Australian and Indian governments. I made a video on the matches between the photos of the Sripuranthan Nataraja and the one the NGA had bought, and released it on YouTube calling it 'Return of the Dancer'. The title turned out to be prophetic!

The campaign gained momentum and was picked up by social media and, more importantly, the Australian mainstream media. It was ABC's programme *Four Corners* which finally tilted the balance. In his interview to ABC, Senator Brandis, who was the attorney general and also minister for the arts, said:

. . . the due diligence standards of the NGA, which are very high – in fact are world's best practice – were not, in my view, sufficiently complied with on this particular occasion. The decision to acquire the object . . . came . . . at a time when there was a sufficient level of doubt about the provenance of the object, that the decision to recommend to the council the acquisition of the object at that time was incautious.[12]

If the reputation of the NGA hadn't been damaged enough there was more embarrassment in store for it. The museum had been consistently maintaining that it had consulted with an expert on Chola art but refused to reveal his or her name. *Four Corners* revealed that the expert the NGA claims to have contacted was Dr Ramachandran Nagaswamy. But Nagaswamy himself categorically denied this! The NGA's chairman himself told *Four Corners* that Dr Nagaswamy had communicated to them that the Nataraja they planned to buy was 'a piece of outstanding quality. He knew of no reason to suspect its provenance.'[13]

But Dr Nagaswamy says this never happened. He never tendered any such advice. Was there an email or a report written by Nagaswamy proving that he supported the NGA's acquisition? No sir, there is not. Why? Because the NGA claims to have been given this advice on a telephone call! A phone call Nagaswamy does not recall participating in.

Dr Nagaswamy stands by his stringent rules on verifying provenances of objects.

'We have always authorized committees consisting of more than three experts to examine all aspects and their views are properly recorded and attested by their signatures before further actions. I know my rules well and do not deviate,' he told the ABC.

The NGA certainly doesn't come out smelling of roses and I'm sure if you had to bet on someone's version of accounts it wouldn't be the NGA's.

That's not all, the ABC programme also revealed that the museum went against its own attorney's advice when it bought the Nataraja – he said the paperwork was 'at best, thin', the NGAs due diligence was 'inadequate', and the available information was 'minimal'.[14] How many red flags were needed for the museum to back off and sound the alarm? The attorney concluded that 'There must be a much deeper enquiry made before title can be confirmed' and even recommended that the museum contact a previous owner, Raj Mehgoub – the same woman who was listed as the previous owner of the Ardhanarishvara as well. In fact, five of the twenty-two pieces that the museum bought from Kapoor between 2002 and 2011 were previously owned by Raj Mehgoub, according to the papers supplied to them by Kapoor. Three were owned by his girlfriend Selina Mohamed and one by his ex-girlfriend Grace Punusamy. Surely the museum should have dug around Raj a little. Had they done this they may have seen that Kapoor's story didn't stand up to even basic scrutiny. In total at least eight objects that Kapoor sold, adding up to $30 million, were claimed to be from the Mehgoub collection. You'd be forgiven for imagining that Raj Mehgoub would be a very posh Chanel-wearing art collector. But what if I told you that Raj, in fact, lived in an ordinary $83,000 house in

Art Of The Past

1242 Madison Avenue New York, NY 10128, Phone (212) 860-7070, Fax (212) 876-5373

LETTER OF PROVENANCE
January 15th 2003

I, Raj Mehgoob, hereby certify that the Dancing Shiva Chola period south India height 51inches was purchased by my husband, Abdulla Mehgoub who was diplomat in Delhi from Sudan during his posting there from 1968 to 1971. This sculpture has been out of India since 1971.

Raj Mehgoub
428 Millbank Road
Upper Darby, PA 19082

E-mail Artofpast@aol.com • www.Artofpast.com

*Letter of provenance for the Sripuranthan Nataraja from
Raj Mehgoub*

Philadelphia up to 2005, when she sold it. Thereafter she moved into another ordinary flat in Queens in New York, not Manhattan where one would expect a collector who had a \$30-million-plus collection would live.

However, the NGA never even tried to contact Mehgoub. The sad story of the Sripuranthan Nataraja and the conduct of the NGA typifies the very worst behaviour of museums.

On 4 September 2014, close to midnight, we received the final confirmation – the Nataraja and Ardhanarishvara were coming home. The call was from Michaela, who had been an invaluable resource on this quest. Australian Prime Minister Tony Abbott would hand it over to his Indian counterpart, Narendra Modi, in New Delhi. Michaela reported: 'The *Australian* understands the Prime Minister decided during a dinner with Attorney-General and Arts Minister George Brandis late last month to bring an end to the saga and present Mr Modi with the idols during his two-day visit.'[15]

Prime Minister Abbott, it is said, wanted to transport the gods on his own plane but they were too heavy and had to be sent to New Delhi in advance. When the Nataraja touched down in New Delhi, he was arriving home after eight years. The Ardhanarishvara had been abroad for over a decade.

This was the first time that the UN convention of 1970 had been put to use between India and Australia.

This was also a watershed moment in the entire Kapoor case and, indeed, a proud moment for us. Physical evidence plays a critical role in such cases and we had now secured some solid proofs. We plunged head on to secure the rest of the evidence.

A senior officer with the Idol Wing, Prateep V. Philip, was quoted as saying, 'The significance of the early return from Australia is that it permits us to have an early trial and prosecution, which will act as a deterrent to global art smugglers.'[16]

It was announced that Dr Nagaswamy, former director of the state archaeology department, and his associates would examine the idols and issue the necessary documents regarding their originality. According to Philip, the verification was a part of the restitution

Narendra Modi and Tony Abbott with the Sripuranthan Nataraja and the Vriddhachalam Ardhanarishvara

Prakash Singh/AFP/Getty Images

process. The same was sent as incontrovertible evidence to Australia.

The Nataraja was taken to the Sripuranthan temple and placed in the same empty niche from where he had been crudely removed. The whole village turned up and the temple was spruced up for the celebration. The village of Sripuranthan had been plunged into darkness eight years ago when its gods had been kidnapped. Now, their Nataraja had come home, and the light had returned to their lives.

12

The Uma in Singapore

From Australia we now head to Singapore where another of the Sripuranthan gods would be discovered in due course.

But first we have to rewind a little, to 2007. The announcer on Singapore's national television was crisp and I wondered how she managed the tough Indian pronunciations. She was telling viewers about the 'Beauty in Asia: 200 BCE to Today' exhibition that would run from 3 May to 23 September 2007 at the ACM in Singapore. 'The highlight of the exhibition will be the unveiling of a bronze Uma Parameshwari dating to the eleventh-century Chola period from Tamil Nadu India,' she said. The museum had just acquired the Sripuranthan Uma from Subhash Kapoor – of course, back in 2007, we didn't even know that the Sripuranthan temple had been robbed. As mentioned earlier, the thefts were only discovered in 2008. I was an aspiring blogger on temple art, new to Singapore, and the opportunity to see and

Sripuranthan Uma

write about the Uma was too good to miss. My wife and I decided to make a day of it and took our son with us.

We got off the Mass Rapid Transit train at the Raffles Place Station one hot Saturday noon. We could see the ACM across the river as we walked past Fullerton Hotel. Soon we were welcomed by massive red cut-outs announcing the exhibition. It was on one such poster that I first saw her. The Chola era Sripuranthan Uma!

This was before the front cameras on mobile phones and the selfie craze, so we simply took a few shots of the brilliantly done posters. The logo of the exhibition and conference was a simple ship motif – my industry. At the exhibition, my heart swelled with pride reading of the maritime pursuits of the Cholas – the Sembians. We climbed the flight of stairs in the stately ACM to the first deck and moved to the inner exhibition area. I turned my head, and there she was.

I had seen quite a few bronzes before, and some almost real, larger-than-life-sized cut-outs of the Uma had lined the passageway of the museum, but nothing had prepared me for seeing her right in front of me. There were no glass cases in those days in special purpose exhibitions (they were installed later). As I pulled out my camera, the guard cautioned me that photography of the main exhibit was not allowed. Though I didn't understand why, I didn't question him. I was caught by her gaze and slowly walked closer.

She looked smaller than the multitude of processional bronzes I had seen across my land like the Vijayanagar ones, but slightly more artistic than the classical tenth-century Chola bronzes that the connoisseur Calambur Sivaramamurthi had lavished his praise on. The detailing of her ornamentation was exquisite – the kandigai (neck ornament), the keyyuram (arm ornament) – everything I had read in the history books had come to life before me. But something was still unique about her. The slender waistline and the delicate turn of the tribhanga, or triple flexion, and the way the spotlights played around the green patina – yes, the patina.

I had seen many examples of the patina on bronzes in museums in India and read all about it. The bronzes under worship never had it. They were too cared for – woken up in the mornings with songs, lovingly bathed, symbolically fed and even sung to sleep with lullabies. They would never develop the patina or bronze rust, which was good for the idol, the scholars said. It stopped further oxidation unlike rust on iron, which devours the metal like cancer. Only in a few odd cases had the patina caused bronze disease. Newspapers featuring finds of buried hoards would have pictures of bronzes that were also very green. But this was very different. The buried ones had lot of encrustations and their coloration was not uniform, like here. I made a mental note to go back and check the archive – the folder was named 'Finds – Hoards'. The security guard was getting nervous and so was the missus. 'It's been ten minutes since you have been staring at her. Come, let us go!' she said.

'Ten minutes? Wah, didn't realize it.'

But I wanted some more. Her kosuvam – where the

end of the sari gets tucked into her waist – I admired the artistry of the sculptor and the way he had draped her sari. The curls of her hair, the flowers flowing over her shoulders, the knot of the yagnopavitha, the sacred thread, just above her chest and then her bewitching smile.

Thirty minutes later my wife was literally dragging me away towards the exit.

I came home that night and blogged about the Uma who had turned me into a statue, riveted and stunned by her exquisite beauty.

> The magnificence of this piece was breathtaking . . . a strange aura of genuine happiness [enveloped me] . . . seeing the handiwork of a gifted artist over 1,000 years ago, surviving and continuing to do its duty – of blending art with spirituality, the mastery of craftsmanship. The statue was at best 2 feet in height, but the detailing was exquisite, the grace and calm of her face and love in the smile, the sharpness of her nose, offsetting the immaculate eyebrows, the enchanting eyes, the lovely locks of her hair falling into rolling tresses over her shoulders, the intricate ornaments on her neck, the grace of her poise – the gentle sway accentuating the narrow waist, the beautiful and elaborate work on her lower garments, her hands and fingers bring life to the figurine, she came to life and I became metal. That is the power that a Chola bronze can wield over you.[1]

I kept returning to see the Uma every few months well into early 2013. It was a strange pull. I dragged friends, relatives, well-wishers away from the oft-repeated Singapore trails of Sentosa and Mustafa and took them to the ACM.

The Uma was by now safely encased in a glass case in the India section on the ground floor and it was difficult to get a reflection-free shot of her. Sometime later, I dragged a friend with his SLR to the museum and he got a great shot of her. Using the photo, I commissioned a portrait of the Uma by an expert artist in Saigon, and she hangs to this day in my room.

Around 2013, the publicity surrounding the Ardhanarishvara match helped in many ways – it upped our profile in social media. We asked members of our community to send us auction house catalogues and art magazines in addition to the image database that they were helping us create. Within weeks of the Ardhanarishvara story we already had every Art of the Past catalogue with us – sourced from old-book shops and libraries.

Then, an American woman – let's call her Ms K to protect her identity, who travels widely in India, visiting offbeat sites and documenting our treasures – sent me a courier. Ms K's contribution to our cause was immense and she's one of two people on the Indic travel circuit whom I genuinely have deep respect and regard for – the other being a Swiss national. Ms K is often the target of trolls who mistake her for an evangelist!

It was late evening when I got home from work and saw the thick envelope. Inside was a whole lot of paper cuttings from glossy magazine advertisements.

Ms K routinely sent me advertisements of Art of the Past which had appeared in the print editions of *Arts of Asia* and *Marg* magazines. The two magazines did not have online versions and were purely subscription based. They wouldn't show up on web searches.

As I contemplated how to proceed with the material in hand, I pulled out my camera and started taking photos of the sheets to capture them digitally for our archive, as a first step.

By the tenth sheet, I was in deep shock. Kapoor had been advertising Chola bronzes, including a Nataraja that we were unaware of, as well as sculptures from every possible state – Odisha, Madhya Pradesh, Gujarat, Karnataka, Kashmir, Goa, Andhra Pradesh. But that's not why I was in shock. Among the clippings there was an Art of the Past advertisement featuring the ACM Uma![2]

I couldn't believe my eyes.

I spent the next fourteen hours mining our archive, feeling bad that the ACM Uma, which was from the Sripuranthan temple, had escaped my eye earlier. After a while I realized why. The original temple photos shot by the IFP, covering Suthamalli and Sripuranthan, had missed out the Uma. But they were covered by a sister organization of the IFP, the École française d'Extrême-Orient, or EFEO, which had merged its collections with the IFP subsequently. The image released by the Idol Wing was so badly resized that it had no resemblance to the ACM Uma, which was purchased by the museum in 2007.

Back in July 2013, I understood the art market relatively less, still having hope in the system, trying to work from within to find solutions. I decided to inform the authorities right away. Reaching out to the Singapore authorities was a bit tricky, and I did this through a good friend. The press coverage of the Vriddhachalam case helped as a good point of reference for my credentials.

I wrote to my friend:

I have been to the Asian Civilisations Museum many times and admired the prized Uma there and was shocked to note that she was purchased from Art of the Past. The plate in the Museum suggests a 2007 date of acquisition. We would be asking for its detailed provenance shortly. I am attaching the magazine advertisement herewith.

Having come to know that the bronze was brought from them, I ran through the Idol Wing website to check their image gallery and found a positive id with the Uma stolen from the Sripuranthan Sivan Temple listed below (3rd image)

http://www.tneow.gov.in/IDOL/status_info.html

...The Uma is very unique in her iconography – and I have run through my entire database and there is no other even remotely similar piece.

I seek your advice on how to intimate this to the ACM and other relevant bodies – as it is clear that the Museum isn't at fault – as the images were put up by the Idol Wing only after their purchase date and prior to that there were no images of the said bronze in public domain or in printed works.

However, it is clear that there is an open case by the Idol Wing which clearly lists this bronze as stolen, stolen by operatives of the Art of the Past, the ACM seems to have purchased the piece from Art of the Past as well.

My friend appeared convinced and forwarded my email and attachments to the higher-ups in the ACM. Sadly, but not surprisingly, the response was in the same tone that many museums have taken recourse to.

Thanks for forwarding this mail and alerting us to its details. The issue has been known to ACM and when they will be approached by official channels, they will have to respond.

ACM has rather stringent provenance verification process put in place however it is very difficult many a times to get more information.

Whatever major pieces we have acquired for the ACM so far are well documented and have run Art Loss Register checks.

Many thanks

So despite knowing that they had a stolen artwork, the ACM took the time-tested option of wait and watch with India, probably hoping that the case against Subhash Kapoor would also lose steam like so many before it.

But they did not contend with Indy.

13

Operation Hidden Idol

Indy rued his chances. He had been preparing a whole dossier on Kapoor since 2009 when he started poking about the curious case of the abandoned container from Mumbai, including the information from the wire taps – remember the small-time buyer of Subhash Kapoor's who confessed to customs violations but was not prosecuted and was instead cultivated as Informant 1? That informant over the years began contacting Kapoor and his associates at Art of the Past, asking for 'fresh' antiquities, or recently stolen objects, while wearing a wire. And so the American authorities knew, thanks to recordings, that Informant 1 was offered two Natarajas for sale in 2011: one for $3.5 million and the other for $5 million. Kapoor said he expected the Natarajas to increase in value by 10–15 per cent every year. One of these, the $5 million Nataraja, is thought to be the Suthamalli Nataraja. Alongside this federal agents knew, through emails obtained by them, that Kapoor was trying to sell two idols of Goddess Parvati for $2.5 million and $3.5 million. The $3.5 million Parvati is thought to be none other than the Suthamalli Sivakami. These are thought to be the four gods that Subhash Kapoor was alluding to in his note to Aaron Freedman in 2011 when he said: 'Give back 4 items to Selina, Bronze dancers which are in the 4 closets.' The total 'value' of these four gods is thought to be $14.5 million.

But just as Indy was about to set the trap for Kapoor, India had suddenly and unexpectedly acted by arresting him in Germany in 2011. A lesser operative would have just dumped the case and moved on.

However, Indy was no ordinary operative. He knew a few token seizures and a couple of high-profile arrests without foolproof legal cases would not solve the problem. He knew the scale and scope of the malaise, probably more than anyone else at that time. He wanted to break up and dismantle the system, expose every wheel, hub and spoke of the international smuggling ring, which viewed such occasional arrests and seizures as the cost of doing business. He wanted to now go after Kapoor's associates in the US and in India, he wanted to smash the supply chain, and also go after the demand side. He wanted to make sure that Kapoor faced justice in the US as well as in India – at worst, if the case against him in India fell apart and, at best, in addition to his convictions in India. He wanted to return to India its lost gods.

And so on 5 January 2012, Indy launched Operation Hidden Idol with the execution of a search warrant for Art of the Past and also one of Kapoor's warehouses.

The initial results were not encouraging, as expected. No antiquities were seized, but some CDs with photographs of statues and shipping records were found. At that time, no one realized how important this seizure would be.

Indy had with him an ocean of information, but it was raw data. The seizure included the handwritten notes that Kapoor had smuggled out to Freedman while he was still in Interpol custody and several addresses of art storages plus transaction lists of major auction houses.

On 26 July 2012, Indy led a raid in a Manhattan storage facility used by Kapoor and netted an estimated $20 million in stolen works. They included Chola era idols reported missing on the Tamil Nadu Idol Wing's website, thought to be stolen in temple raids.

HSI invited the local affiliate of NBC to broadcast footage of the agents hauling away several trucks of booty, including a 1600 pound Shakyamuni Buddha from the Chola period, which required an entire truck of its own.

In October 2012, there was another raid in the Pierre, New York. Agents hauled off a bust of a Bodhisattva, which were believed to be from the third century, and a tenth-century white sandstone Ganesha. Kapoor had lent the statues to the hotel.

On 5 December 2012, at the port of Newark, the final raid of the year netted another five Chola era statues, including another Parvati linked to Kapoor and listed as stolen by Interpol.

The full information of all the seizures and the first official photos were released on the US Immigrations

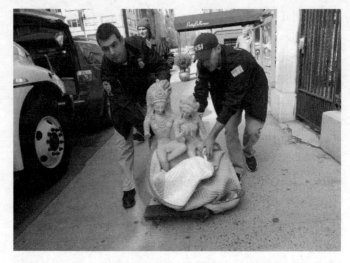

Operation Hidden Idol in progress

and Customs Enforcement website thereafter. There were raids in a total of six locations. Overall 2622 items were recovered, valued in Kapoor's books (mostly on 2006–09 costs) at a whopping $107,682,000! As mentioned earlier, this was just his holding stock or inventory in known storage locations. Kapoor had been in business for thirty-five years. You do the maths on what the lifetime value of the loot would add up to. Jason put this figure in perspective for the shocked art world. He wrote in 2012, 'The FBI's art squad has seized a total of $150 million in art since its inception in 2004.' In the Kapoor case, $100 million of art was recovered in just a few months.[1]

There was a picture of HSI Special Agent-in-Charge James Hayes posing with five seized Chola bronzes on the ICE website. He was quoted as saying:

Subhash Kapoor's alleged smuggling of cultural artefacts worth more than an estimated US$100 million makes him one of the most prolific commodities smugglers in the world today. We urge the art community to help us identify artefacts sold or donated by Subhash Kapoor so that we can ensure their legitimacy. We will continue to work with our law enforcement partners and the government of India to bring Mr Kapoor to justice and return the artefacts in question to their rightful owners. HSI understands full-well that for many nations there is no price tag when it comes to their national treasures.

I'd just like to reiterate one point that Hayes made. Art crime is not a 'soft' matter. It's not something that should be relegated to the 'features' or 'arts' pages of newspapers. It's in the same league as drugs, arms and gold smuggling. Art crime is crime. Art smuggling is smuggling. And make no mistake, according to American law enforcement, Subhash Kapoor was 'one of the most prolific commodities smugglers in the world'.

This news was also covered by Jason Felch on his website chasingaphrodite.com with a special interview. In the interview, Hayes urged collectors and museums that had purchased objects from Kapoor to come forward and notify the investigators. He said:

We ask that those collectors contact us. Our investigation is on-going and we're looking to confirm the legitimacy of those objects. We have already received several calls from law firms representing people who had acquired pieces through Kapoor and were concerned about whether they were in possession of stolen goods.[2]

But no major museum or collector volunteered with information. They had spent millions on their acquisitions, based on poor, cosmetic due diligence, and were willing to stick it out, pinning their hope on India's past record of shabby prosecution, non-existent follow-up and short memory.

Meanwhile, as promised by Indy, he also started going after Kapoor's associates. On 4 December 2013, a charge sheet was filed in a New York court against Aaron Freedman, Kapoor's assistant and manager at Art of the Past. Among other things, the charge sheet said: 'He [Freedman] arranged for the shipping into and out of the United States of antiquities stolen from numerous countries including, but not limited to, India, Afghanistan, Pakistan, and Cambodia, having the antiquities shipped through intermediaries in order to create documentation to help launder the pieces. He also arranged for the manufacturing of false provenances for illicit cultural property, the contacting of prospective buyers, and the ultimate sale and transport of these looted and thereafter laundered antiquities.' Freedman was charged with conspiracy and possession of stolen goods. The charge sheet specifically mentioned the

Sripuranthan Nataraja that went to the NGA – and also, much to the annoyance of the officials at the ACM in Singapore, the Sripuranthan Uma:

> During the period from on or about January 2005 to November 2006, one Uma Parameshvari (known as the '$650,000 Uma for Singapore'), owned by the Central Government of India, was stolen from the Sivan Temple in India's Ariyalur District [the Sripuranthan temple]. During the period January 2006 to on or about January 2007, defendant [that is, Freedman] and other co-conspirators shipped the $650,000 Uma for Singapore, from India to the United States. On or about February 2007, defendant and other co-conspirators arranged for the sale and transport of the $650,000 Uma to the Asian Civilisations Museum in Singapore.[3]

Its hand forced by the Americans, in January 2014 the ACM acknowledged it had purchased a total of thirty objects from Kapoor. However, the ACM did not name the objects nor detail their provenance nor disclose the price paid for them.

The total value of the ACM's acquisitions from Kapoor was later found to be $1,328,250. There were quite a few problematic pieces, including Amaravathi stupa fragments, a Nagapattinam bronze Buddha and several Chandraketugarh rattles.

Faced with mounting pressure and evidence, the museum had no choice but to return the Sripuranthan Uma to India on 6 November 2015, while there was status quo on the rest of the Kapoor objects at the ACM. Like the NGA, the ACM has also sued Subhash Kapoor for reimbursement of money they had spent on objects with cooked-up provenances.

In a curious twist, Freedman pleaded guilty to conspiracy and possession of stolen property in court. He had been working for Kapoor since 1995, after graduating from Vassar College and then studying history of art at Rutgers University. His lawyer made conciliatory statements to the press, including that Freedman wanted to 'take concrete steps to rectify his serious mistakes'.[4] The prosecutor also extended a friendly hand, telling a reporter, 'Mr Freedman, I believe, is sincerely and genuinely remorseful and repentant and he has taken significant steps toward making amends.' It didn't surprise anyone that Freedman was now cooperating with investigators. He had turned on Kapoor.

14

The Toledo Ganesha

Invigorated by the success on the ACM Uma match, and shocked that I had missed making the connection for so long, in 2013 I pushed data mining and started running a check on every museum purchase of Chola bronzes back to 2006. I got a random hit – the Toledo Museum of Art in Ohio had purchased a Ganesha in 2006, with object number 2006.37. I suspected it to be from the Sripuranthan temple. It was late night on 18 July 2013 when I emailed Jason and the journalist Srivathsan from *The Hindu* about my suspicions. I asked Srivathsan for high resolution pictures from the IFP of the Sripuranthan Ganesha and Jason to put us through to the museum authorities.

Jason sent an email to Brian Kennedy, director of the Toledo Museum of Art in Ohio, giving a copy of the police report showing a blurry image of the stolen Ganesha. He requested for the details of the Ganesha's ownership history, as well as the forty-four objects Toledo

Sripuranthan Ganesha

had acquired from Subhash Kapoor, for which he had
sought information a year ago.

The problem was we still needed both the source photo
from the IFP and a high resolution photo from Toledo
for a match. Thankfully, we didn't have to rely on the
museum officials. Social media again came to our rescue.
A good friend, who is also a technocrat and author, Ravi
Venugopal, volunteered to drive down to Toledo. The
photos arrived in three days.

Meanwhile, we managed to access the Toledo Museum
of Art Annual Report of 2007. It contained a list of gifts
from Subhash Kapoor. There were over fifty items, mainly
small terracottas from the Gupta period and many more
from Chandraketugarh. And to top it there was this
donation as well:

The Museum recognizes and thanks the following
organizations, businesses, and individuals who made
gifts during 2008 in support of art acquisitions, capital
projects, and special programs:

$100,000+ – Subhash Kapoor: gift of art
Cumulative Giving
The Toledo Museum of Art salutes the following
donors for their generosity and continuing support
during its second century:
$250,000 to $499,999 – Mr Subhash Kapoor

Why would a dealer, who sold a bronze Ganesha for
$245,000, gift them almost half a million in cash and
kind? Obviously Kapoor's business was so large that a

gift worth half a million dollars was a justified incidental expense. (It is pertinent to mention here that in no way am I trying to imply that any of the museums or curators I've mentioned took gifts, donations or inducements from Subhash Kapoor as quid pro quo to cover up for him, accept shoddy provenances, or turn a blind eye to items that they knew to be stolen. There is no proof of intentional wrongdoing on the part of any of the museums – whether the Toledo Museum, the ACM, the NGA, the AGNSW, or any other. However, what is likely is that the continuous stream of clever gifts from Subhash Kapoor must have earned him enough goodwill to lessen the suspicion of museums, even caused their guard to be lowered a bit. The provenance checks conducted by museums were certainly found wanting.)

We finally received a churlish, rude response from the museum after five days.

Mr Felch:

We have received your email to Dr Kennedy dated 7/18/2013. We will investigate the information you have provided in regard to the Ganesha (TMA 2006.37).

In regards to the 44 objects you refer to acquired by TMA as gifts from Subhash Kapoor, we informed the *New York Times* (see Museums Studying Dealer's Artefacts, July 27, 2012) that these were small terra cotta objects of minor value. They are not on display at the Museum but have been used for teaching purposes.

Our policy is to respond to requests about objects in the TMA collections made by official authorities such as museums, law enforcement agencies, foreign governments and those making legal claims to ownership. There have been no such inquiries to date in regard to the objects referred to in your email.

Basically a polite way of telling us to take a hike, get lost, and mind our own business.

Ravi kept his promise and sent the high resolution photos over the weekend. We were in luck – two blemishes made our task easier.

The process of making a bronze involves the idol first being fashioned in wax and then coated in clay. Once the clay hardens it's fired and the wax melts away. The original wax sculpture is lost forever, leaving a hollow core inside the clay mould. Into this clay mould is poured molten metal. Once the metal cools the clay mould is broken to reveal the sculpture.

Critical to our work of matching, for instance, the original IFP photos of the Sripuranthan Ganesha to the Toledo Museum's Ganesha, is the fact that since the mould cannot be reused, every cast is unique – like a fingerprint. Every bronze has unique signatures – minor breaks in some cases or small blemishes.

In the case of the Toledo Ganesha, the elephant god had two small blemishes. Years ago, when the wax sculpture was made, the artist perhaps nicked the wax body with his fingernail, leaving a blemish. Or maybe the imperfection was the result of the way the metal was poured. Be that as it may, the two imperfections of the Ganesha had been miraculously captured in the

IFP photographs and were there in plain sight in Ravi's photos. We had a perfect match.

Though the museum remained defiant to our emails, the wheels had started moving inside the system. We were not aware of this and started a Facebook and YouTube campaign. Knowing that Toledo was a sister city of Coimbatore in India, a Facebook group was started asking to remove Toledo as a sister city of Coimbatore. The YouTube video was titled 'Remover of Obstacles'.

Finally, in February 2014 the museum released this statement:

Subhash Kapoor Acquisitions Under Review

The Toledo Museum of Art, like many museums across the country, acquired objects from Mr Kapoor in the period from 2001–2010. The most significant of the eight acquired by the Toledo Museum of Art from Mr Kapoor is a Ganesha figure. After the 2006 Ganesha purchase, Mr Kapoor gifted 56 small terracotta idols to the Museum. The purchased items have been on public display. The gifted items have never been on public display.

On July 18, 2013, the Museum received a copy of an Indian police report that includes photographs of 18 metal idols stolen from Sripuranthan Village in Tamil Nadu. One of the images of a Ganesha figure closely resembles the Ganesha purchased by the Museum in 2006 from Art of the Past. At the time of purchase consideration, the Museum received a provenance affidavit and the curator personally spoke to the listed previous owner. The object was also run through the Art Loss Registry with no issues detected.

On July 24, 2013, TMA Director Brian Kennedy sent a letter to the Consulate General of India in New York, Mr Sugandh Rajaram, requesting his assistance in researching the Ganesha's provenance with Indian officials. To date, the Museum has received no response.

On February 17, 2014, a letter was sent to Dr S. Jaishankar, Ambassador of India to the United States, soliciting his assistance. The Museum has not been contacted by Immigration and Customs Enforcement or any other U.S. or foreign government agency in regards to this object and others the Museum purchased from Art of the Past or gifted by Mr Kapoor.

The statement also carried copies of the letters sent by the museum to the Indian authorities in the US, to which it did not receive any response! Here we were trying our hardest, burning the midnight oil while juggling day jobs and families to protect our heritage, but the Indian authorities didn't even bother to follow up on such critical communications.

The Toledo Museum had acquired the Ganesha soon after it was stolen in May 2006, for $245,000. It maintained that proper due diligence had been conducted, including a provenance affidavit – a letter dated 2 January 2006 on the Art of the Past letterhead. It carried a claim by Selina Mohamed stating that she had inherited the sculpture from her mother, Rajpati Singh Mohamed, who had bought it on a trip to India in 1971 – before

Art Of The Past

1242 Madison Avenue New York, NY 10128, Phone (212) 860-7070, Fax (212) 876-5373

LETTER OF PROVENANCE
Jan 2nd 2006

I, Selina Mohamed, hereby certify that the Dancing Ganesha bronze Chola period size approximately 20 inch from South India, was purchased by my Mother, Rajpati Singh Mohamad in 1971 while on there travel to India My parents' families were originally from India, but settled in British Guyana several generations ago. We have been living in New York since 1971. I inherited these sculpture from my mother. It has been in my possession since that time.

Selina Mohamed
119-49 Union Turnpike, Apartment #8E
Forest Hills, New York 11375
(718) 261-6928

E-mail Artofpast@aol.com • www.Artofpast.com

Letter of provenance from Selina Mohamed for the
Sripuranthan Ganesha

the Antiquities and Art Treasures Act, 1972 had been passed in India. Selina claimed the sculpture had been in her possession in New York since then.

Selina was found to have issued many such fake

provenance letters to aid Subhash Kapoor. She also had three warehouses in her name, where the illegal artefacts were stored, which warehouses were paid for by Subhash Kapoor.

So the Toledo Museum's meticulous process of due diligence basically relied on a sheet of paper that turned out to be a fake.

Time and again we came up against the same kind of 'optical' due diligence – a fake receipt dated prior to 1970, a fake provenance claiming ownership, and a certificate from ALR. And of course a 'gullible' museum willing to believe without any scepticism the stories fed to it by dealers.

Finally, in October 2014, the museum handed over the Ganesha to ICE, USA. In June 2016, the Ganesha was formally handed over to the Indian prime minister, Narendra Modi, in a formal ceremony, along with some other items. Another one of our gods had been brought back home.

There were other discoveries of antiquities related to Subhash Kapoor, too, and many are the people who have been involved in identifying them and helping to bring them back to India. It isn't possible to recount all those unbelievable stories here. But I would be remiss if I didn't mention in particular the work of Dr Kirit Mankodi, a rare academic committed to protecting India and her heritage. It is thanks to him and his tireless efforts that the pan-Indian nature of Subhash Kapoor's operation has come to be understood. This isn't a problem that plagues Tamil Nadu and other southern states alone. The loot of our gods is taking place in temples across the land, from Kashmir to Kanyakumari.

15

The Associates

Indy and I had been in touch electronically all these years and from a few random emails it was becoming an almost daily interaction. So when I received an email from him saying he was planning to visit Chennai and asked if I could make it down from Singapore, I couldn't wait. I made my way to Chennai in September 2013 to secretly meet him. No one knew the purpose of my trip. As far as my family was concerned – and I apologize through this disclosure to them – I was away on official work.

I waited for Indy to show up at the lobby of the hotel, looking out for the man with his signature baseball cap. It was ironical that we met at the recently opened Grand Chola Hotel. Indy had just come back after a frustrating meeting with the Idol Wing and was planning a visit to the temple theft sites later during the week and to the IFP in Puducherry but we had half of Saturday and a full day on Sunday to talk before I headed back to Singapore.

The Idol Wing also introduced their expert Dr Nagaswamy to Indy as the man who helped make the different matches that were crucial to authenticate the Australian Nataraja as the Sripuranthan Nataraja. Indy shot back, 'But hadn't Vijay from Singapore done this months back and put it up online?' It apparently shocked them as they were not aware of our little collaboration on the side.

After a few cups of coffee we headed to his hotel room. We recollected months of online exchanges – and then, for the first time I saw the Kapoor dossier. Indy showed me just a sample of the treasure trove so painstakingly harvested from countless hours of sieving through thousands of emails and photographs seized during the Operation Hidden Idol raids. If not for the sabotage on Sanjeevi Asokan's computer, we would have had a similar Sanjeevi dossier.

Indy had access to hundreds if not thousands of robber photos, some going back even to the 1980s. My heart sank and eyes watered as I peered at the grainy polaroids, black-and-white prints and later colour photos of the very best of Indian art – in dingy, shady environs, in the hands of robbers as they posed with their booty, freshly dug up antiquities, mud and dirt still clinging to them – both as proof of their genuineness and their antiquity. These photos were then sent out to prospective buyers.

I made a simple request to Indy. I asked for just a hundred of those robber photos of antiquities that Subhash Kapoor had passed on and not bought. I was sure that Kapoor would be dealt with by the courts – my belief in Indian law enforcement and judiciary was and is still high – but here we had a unique door to the illicit antiquities market. We had the password to an Aladdin's cave of traffickers.

I wasn't sure of the task I had taken on. The Italians had fine-tuned matching robber photos to an art form – their Comando Carabinieri per la Tutela del Patrimonio Culturale – Carabinieri TPC for short – had the best sleuths, trained eyes and the latest computer technology which included structured archives, databases and image-matching software.

I had my trusted HP laptop and the support of social media and a team of energetic volunteers. We had built our database for free and now it was time to see if it worked. The challenge was: take a robber photo of an item that Subhash Kapoor had declined to purchase and find out where that antiquity was now – with a dealer or museum. Then we could go after them to get it back and make the dealer and supplier both face justice.

The hours and years of reading, visiting sites, and discussing sculptural styles with fellow members of Facebook groups had equipped me. The robbers' choices aided me as well – they had targeted the very best of Indian art. I spread out my work on my father's forty-year-old dining table that Saturday evening. The robber photos started speaking to me – I am Gupta dynasty, I am eighth century, I am from Madhya Pradesh, I am Pala dynasty, I am from Odisha ...

In just under eight hours I had cracked over twenty of the 100 cases. I had managed to trace the antiquities using our database of museum collections, auction house catalogues and dealer advertisements. We had more than a dozen shady dealers, auction houses and museums in our grasp. They were the people who were creating demand. They were the ones who bought the pieces that Kapoor had declined to buy.

Indy and I met again the next morning. Over the next sixteen hours we had cracked the code. We were dealing with not a single gang of thieves but a network of many specialized gangs, we realized.

Armed with this information Indy kicked off Phase 2 of Operation Hidden Idol – getting the associates.

As part of the operation, the American investigative team had meetings with the Idol Wing and gave them part of the Kapoor dossier – emails, shipping documents, robber photos and details of bank transfers – so that they could act on Kapoor's Indian contacts. After all, the Americans couldn't launch operations on Indian soil. They needed the Idol Wing to do some of the lifting. It was a signed handover duly acknowledged by the Idol Wing.

Inside the dossier were details of two major operators – Deendayal and Sanjeevi. Amongst other things, there were photos of Deendayal's offerings of antiquities for sale as well as another crucial piece of evidence. One that should have got him arrested right away.

It was an invoice and note from the Sanjeevi-associated Selva Exports to Subhash Kapoor's Nimbus dated 18 January 2007.

The note read:

Sir,

Please find herewith our Banker's details for the payment by Swift Transfer instructed by Mr Deena Dayal towards the Export of your order goods. We request you to send us the payment for USD 11,400.

SELVA EXPORTS

16, Aravamudha Garden Street, Behind Dasaprakash Hotel, Egmore, Chennai - 600 008, India
Phone : 0091-44-28253033 Fax : 0091 - 44 - 28238967
E-mail : selvaexp@sify.com, artcolony@sify.com

TO

Date 18-1-2007

NIMBUS IMPORT & EXPORT INC
U.S.A.
E-mail: artofpast@aol.com ✓

Sir,

Please find herewith our Banker's Details for the payment by Swift Transfer instructed by Mr. Deena Dayal towards the Export of your order goods. We request you to send us the payment for **USD 11,400.**

OUR BANKER'S DETAILS

1. REMITTER : **NIMBUS IMPORT & EXPORT INC U.S.A.**

2. REMITTER'S CONNECTING SWIFT CODE BANKER : BOFAUS3N BANK OF AMERICA, 100 WEST AB.NO.026009593 33RD STREET, 4TH FLOOR, NEWYORK.NY 10018.

3. CONNECTING BANKER'S ACCOUNT NUMBER : 6550-5-91876

4. RECEIVER : SELVA EXPORTS SOUTH INDIA.

5. RECEIVER'S BANK : SWIFT:**CNRBINBBMFD** **A/C.NO.10221** OF **SELVA EXPORTS** CANARA BANK, KILPAUK BRANCH, CHENNAI-600 010.

Thanking you,
"BEST REGARDS"

Yours sincerely,
for SELVA EXPORTS.

Invoice and note from the Sanjeevi-associated Selva Exports to Subhash Kapoor's Nimbus

The invoice copy was handed over in late September 2014 to the Idol Wing. But, shock of shocks, nothing happened.

In July 2015, Indy followed this up with another round of information sharing with the Indian authorities. This time he shared evidence against Vallabh Prakash and his son Aditya. He is the Kapoor associate who's said to have facilitated, among other things, the export of the AGNSW Ardhanarishvara from India. His name also figures in the hand-cut Nataraja case. And also in the note that Kapoor wrote to Aaron asking him to strike a 'deal' with the Indian authorities. Again, nothing happened. The Indians were just sitting pretty.

The long delay by India to seek restitution of the Subhash Kapoor–related objects that were being identified and, in many cases, seized all over the world was hurting mine and my colleagues' morale. Sporadic returns had happened from Singapore, Australia, Germany and Canada, but the Indian law enforcement agencies were not doing much to go after the actual culprits, despite being given clear evidence.

Nevertheless luck or providence continued to support our quest and we couldn't get bogged down by the poor pace of progress in India. The image banks, emails and other information obtained from the Operation Hidden Idol raids on Kapoor's offices and warehouses were yielding more and more matches. Through the information that the Americans had access to, they were able to identify a number of 'networks' of thieves and smugglers that specialized in particular areas of art. There is, for instance, a Gandharan network that operates in Pakistan and Afghanistan, a Himalayan network run by a man of Tibetan origin who lives between Nepal and Hong Kong and who smuggles illicit pieces out of Nepal. The Americans were able to identify three more such networks. But crucially they were able to arrest and legally move against one of the most high-profile and respected dealers in the international art scene: Nancy Wiener. This was the most talked about arrest after Subhash Kapoor's and caused an earthquake in the art world.

Nancy ran the prestigious and glittering Wiener Gallery after her mother Doris passed away in 2011 at the ripe old age of 88. Doris was raised in New York and married a prominent jewellery designer. She began travelling to India in 1966 and from the late 1960s began selling Indian art – sculpture and paintings – in New York at sale exhibitions. Doris's clients were the cream of American society and included John D. Rockefeller III, Igor Stravinksy and Jacqueline Kennedy. According to her obituary in the *New York Times*, 'Iconic works of art from the Doris Wiener Gallery formed the basis of many major museum collections of Asian art world-wide. These include the Metropolitan Museum of Art, the Cleveland Museum of Art, the Norton Simon Museum of Art, Asia Society and the Brooklyn Museum, among others.' Christie's auction house called Doris 'one of the most distinguished tastemakers in this collecting category'.[1] To be honest, I'm not sure I'd take that as a compliment. Nancy took over the business and the prestigious collection after her mother died.

But little did people know that American law enforcement had long suspected that the Wiener Gallery had links with Vaman Narayan Ghiya, an Indian who was arrested in 2003 in Jaipur for possession of stolen goods and trafficking in looted antiquities. Ghiya was at first convicted and sentenced to life in prison but was later acquitted by a high court because the police seriously bungled the investigation.[2]

In 1997, the British journalist Peter Watson published a book, *Sotheby's: The Inside Story*, exposing the auction house and its problematic relationship with Vaman Ghiya. The fallout was so severe that Sotheby's actually closed its London antiquities department – which was the focus of the exposé – and moved those operations to New York. The Sotheby's employee who had links to Ghiya left the firm but curiously several objects associated with Ghiya kept coming up for sale at auctions in the US conducted by Sotheby's and Christie's.[3] Whenever the auction houses would be questioned on this, they would deny that the objects had anything to do with Ghiya and would say that the items had been consigned by 'a prominent New York dealer'. We all wondered who this was. Some people in the know were suspicious that it was Doris Wiener.

The breakthrough in the case came in the form of three robber photos of a Kushan era Buddha in the Kapoor archive. The photos were found in a folder titled Shantoo. The idol was a perfect match with a Buddha in the ACM Singapore – complete with its pedestal inscription and the Bodhi tree carved on the reverse.

According to later court documents, the Buddha was bought by Wiener from Vaman Ghiya who 'often used Shantoo to sell looted antiquities'.[4] But at that time no matter how much we pressed the ACM for information on the ownership history of the Buddha they refused to divulge anything. We still do not have access to the provenance documentation supplied to the museum at the time of the purchase from Wiener.

Interestingly, a very similar Buddha to the one in the ACM that we suspected to also be from the Wiener Gallery was on display at the, by now notorious, NGA. Of course the intrepid and indefatigable Jason and Michaela were already on that case! Jason had received an anonymous tip alerting him to the fact that the transaction history of the Buddha was dodgy.

But as usual, getting information out of the NGA was tedious and tiring. The museum's spokesperson wholly rejected Michaela's request for provenance information. When Michaela appealed against this and filed a freedom of information request, she was supplied with a provenance in which the names of people had been redacted! Nevertheless, we ultimately confirmed that, as suspected, the Buddha had been sold to the museum by the Wiener Gallery. (It must be mentioned that the museum's reluctance to part with the information caused a 14-month delay.)

When the temperatures started to rise, the NGA got in touch with the expert, Donald Stadtner, who had authenticated the sculpture for the Wiener Gallery. Shockingly, they hadn't done this at the time of the purchase. The expert told the museum's curator that while he was sure the statue wasn't a fake, he also believed the idol to have been stolen from India and the provenance to be cooked up!

At the time of the $1 million-plus purchase, the NGA curators had not checked the provenance provided by Nancy Wiener; instead they opted to swallow whole her story of its history. Could this have been avoided? Hell, yes.

Two years earlier, in 2005, Canada's Royal Ontario Museum had been offered the same statue but they had declined to buy it because the curator actually did their job and contacted the expert who had authenticated the statue for Wiener. Stadtner, an authority on Indian art, said the piece was genuine but that he thought it had been exported illegally and bogus paperwork had been created to give it authenticity.

Guess what happened next? Nancy Wiener refunded the NGA its money, took the Buddha back, and then 'donated' it to India. But the uncomfortable questions weren't about to go away.

This was in 2014. I was itching for action over the next two years and constantly pushing Indy to swoop in and move against Wiener. But as a trained operator, he bid his time.

We were in luck. Every year there is 'a collaboration of top-tier Asian art specialists, major auction houses, and world-renowned museums and Asian cultural institutions in the metropolitan New York area' to 'celebrate and promote Asian art'.[5] During the Asia Week in 2016,

Kushan Buddha

Nancy offered for sale an object for which we had robber photos from the Kapoor archive.

Indy went for the kill. He raided the Wiener Gallery and seized the object, and two other dodgy items, and 'confiscated thousands of documents and emails'.[6] Indy conducted four other raids on Asia Week exhibitors over that week and seized more than $20 million worth of antiques. This was all thanks to data coming out of Kapoor's business records and archive.

Among other raids, the famed auction house Christie's was also targeted and two items were confiscated from the collection of the London doctor Avijit Lahiri that the auction house was about to put under the hammer. Those objects, according to court records, were connected to Subhash Kapoor. It was none other than Shantoo, again, who had sent Kapoor robber photos of the two Lahiri collection objects surrounded by grass and mud, evidently shortly after they had been stolen.

An aside about Christie's auction house and its practices: according to court documents in the case *The People of the State of New York* v *Nancy Wiener*, Christie's policy 'requires only that an antiquity have been out of its country of origin prior to 2000 (or 1999 for Cambodia), regardless of that country's patrimony law'. I'm not sure what more evidence one requires on the ordering of priorities of this famed auctioneer.

By moving against traffickers during Asia Week, the Cannes of the Asian art circuit, we had successfully taken the war to the heart of the art world.

'This seizure at the beginning of an international event as well recognized as Asia Week New York sends two important messages,' Angel M. Melendez, special agent in charge of HSI New York, said in a release. 'First and foremost, it demonstrates that we are committed to protecting cultural heritage around the world and second, it demonstrates that we are monitoring the market to protect prospective buyers as well.'[7]

The raids and media pressure were yielding beautiful rewards. Now museums and dealers were handing over items more easily. When I spotted a Chola bronze at the Ball State Museum in Indiana and investigations revealed that it was indeed bought from Kapoor, the museum voluntarily handed it over to the HSI. A private dealer handed over the Sripuranthan Manickavasagar, the ninth-century Tamil poet-saint, in New York. Similarly we found matches from the Kapoor archive to items in the Peabody Essex Museum, the Harn Museum, and the Honolulu Museum! Faced with imminent seizures the museums handed over the artefacts.

But what about India? How could we force the Indian authorities to act on the information that they had? It was at this time, in 2016, that Indy and I met again. Prime Minister Modi was due to make a much publicized first visit as prime minister to the US in June 2016. It was a God-sent opportunity. I asked Indy if we could play a small game. Would it be possible for the US to return an important number of idols during the visit? India had that far got back 17 idols since 1972. Twenty would be a very good number for the US to return. Indy responded, 'Why 20, we will return 200.'

Yes, the US side offered to return 200 items – in what would be a historic occasion – and the date of 7 June was set for the ceremonial handover. It was included in the official schedule of the prime minister's visit.

In early May we made our move – the US side refused to go ahead with the restitution as Indian law enforcement agencies had not shown enough action, they said.

Things went into a tizzy. Senior officials from the Ministry of External Affairs scrambled to find a solution in the face of such an embarrassing U-turn and slap on the face. Officials from the Tamil Nadu Idol Wing and Mumbai personally flew to New York where I presume they faced some uncomfortable questions.

On 27 May the delegation returned to India carrying two small bronzes as a symbol of American goodwill and proof of what was in store – if they acted fast and moved on the information that was with them.

On 30 May, the Idol Wing finally raided Deendayal's posh house in a premier neighbourhood in the heart of Chennai. The raid yielded over 300 idols and paintings. Deendayal himself surrendered to the cops after a couple of days. His close associate Narasimhan who ran an antique shop in the seaside heritage town of Mamallapuram was arrested in the following weeks. He had a 100,000 quare foot warehouse in Mamallapuram and found buried underneath were

Idols recovered after the raid on Deendayal's home

Arun Sankar/AFP/Getty Images

more bronzes. Both had several cases of idol theft pending against them for over a decade – including the hand-cut Nataraja case.

The ceremony with Prime Minister Modi went ahead as planned. On glittering display were the Sripuranthan Ganesha and the Sripuranthan Manickavasagar amongst other gods – a total of eight artefacts were presented to Modi.

The headlines declared that the US had returned over 200 artefacts worth more than $100 million to India.[8] But sadly the balance of the 200 have been caught in the ASI's red tape. What an anticlimax!

In November 2016, the Directorate of Revenue Intelligence (DRI) and the Idol Wing finally arrested Vallabh and Aditya Prakash. Originally from Nepal, they moved to Mumbai in 1959. They were officially charged with smuggling the AGNSW Ardhanarishvara.

In December 2016, Nancy Wiener was arrested by the US authorities in New York and charged with criminal possession of stolen property and conspiring with international smuggling networks to buy, smuggle, launder and sell stolen art. There are two things that stand out in particular in the case registered against Nancy.

One, the official complaint against Wiener gives us a glimpse into the five international art crime networks with which she is accused of having conspired. These are the aforementioned Himalayan network and Gandharan network, and the Om Sharma network (according to the complaint Sharma is 'a supplier of illicit antiquities from India'), the Sharod Singh network (Singh is also described in the complaint as 'a supplier of illicit antiquities from India') and the Vaman Narayan Ghiya network.[9]

Two, court documents reveal the identity of Subhash Kapoor's trusted Shantoo: 'According to a former employee of Kapoor, "Shantoo" is the nickname of Ranjeet Kanwar, one of Kapoor's main suppliers of stolen antiquities from India.'[10] Remember, Shantoo is repeatedly mentioned by Subhash in his notes to Aaron asking for a 'deal' to be struck with Indian officials. He's also, according to court documents, involved in the ACM Buddha case and in the objects from the Lahiri collection that were seized from Christie's by the US authorities during Asia Week.

Sadly, despite all this hard work Indy was reassigned from the Kapoor case in December 2016. The Wiener case was his final salvo, his swan song. India owes him a tremendous debt of gratitude. He understands and cares more deeply about Indian heritage and culture than most Indians I know.

16

The Nataraja and Uma Hidden in New York

We have now seen how after Kapoor's arrest and the seizure of his papers the Indian and American authorities were able to proceed against several of Kapoor's associates. In India, Deendayal was arrested and is under trial (though he's out on bail now), Vallabh and Aditya Prakash are in jail, awaiting trial, and Sanjeevi Asokan is back in jail after being released on bail and new charges have been added to those already against him relating to the Sripuranthan and Suthamalli robberies. Kader Batcha of the Idol Wing was finally arrested on 14 September 2017, after an intervention by the Madras High Court, and after being on the run for months – imagine a top police official on the run from the law![1] The Indian police haven't yet acted on the disclosures made by the US authorities in which they identified Shantoo as Ranjeet Kanwar.

In the US, Aaron Freedman pleaded guilty and is cooperating with the authorities, and Nancy Wiener was arrested though she's now out on bail while her trial continues. But as we near the end of our story, you must be wondering whatever happened to Subhash's girlfriend Selina Mohamed and his sister Sushma Sareen?

But before we go into that I'd like to take you back to the note that Subhash sent Aaron from Germany in which he said 'Give back 4 items to Selina, Bronze dancers which are in the 4 closets'. That note was dated 3 November 2011. In a subsequent note to Aaron on 6 November 2011, Subhash clarified, '4 dancers bronze in 4 closets = 2 pairs nataraj & conserts [sic]'. As mentioned earlier, these missives to Aaron were recovered during the Operation Hidden Idol raids. Also, as mentioned before, we know through Indy's Informant 1 that Kapoor had been trying to sell two Natarajas for $3.5 million and $5 million each. In addition, Kapoor had been trying to sell two Parvatis for $2.5 million and $3.5 million each. The $5 million Nataraja is thought to be the inscribed Suthamalli Nataraja we first encountered in Chapter 1 and the $3.5 million Parvati is thought to be his pair, the inscribed Suthamalli Sivakami. You will recall that it was the discovery of these Suthamalli inscribed bronzes in Subhash Kapoor's gallery through an anonymous tip that was one of the tipping points in the case against him.

Around the time that Aaron Freedman was charge-sheeted by the authorities in 2013, Selina Mohamed was also charged with possession of stolen property, referring to the four bronze idols that Subhash Kapoor had asked her to hide, and also with conspiring to launder stolen antiquities, creating false ownership histories, etc.

Selina pleaded guilty to the conspiracy charge as part of a plea agreement with the authorities. Cultural heritage lawyer Rick St Hilaire explains:

> Mohamed pleaded guilty in December 2013 to a misdemeanor charge of conspiracy in the fifth degree, which is the intent to commit a felony with one or more persons. The prosecution dropped felony charges of criminal possession of stolen property as part of a negotiated plea agreement.
>
> ... [In 2015] the court handed down a sentence that consisted of a conditional discharge. The conditional discharge means that Mohamed must remain of good behavior for one year or face court-imposed sanctions.[2]

But why did the authorities drop the possession of stolen property charge? According to court documents, Aaron moved the four idols to Selina's apartment, as directed by Subhash Kapoor. However, after the Operation Hidden Idol raids began on 5 January 2012, 'Selina Mohamed no longer wanted the four stolen bronzes kept in her apartment. It was arranged with ... Sushma Sareen that the four bronzes would be picked up and moved to a "safe location" ... Sareen made the shipping arrangements. In fact, [an] informant ... wanted the stolen statues returned to the gallery, but Sushma Sareen stated that they would [be] safer with her.'[3]

So the four bronze idols are currently apparently with Sushma Sareen, not with Selina.

Sushma was also charged in 2013 for possession of stolen property. The complaint against her additionally states, 'According to [an] informant . . . defendant [Sushma Sareen] has been closely involved with the illegal business of Art of the Past since Kapoor's arrest . . . She has travelled to India, assisted with wire transfers, and contacted antiquities smugglers with prior dealings with Kapoor.'[4] Sushma Sareen has denied all charges and is currently out on bail – on a $10,000 bond, when she has been accused of being in possession of idols worth $14.5 million, but which are in fact priceless. India has taken no action to bring separate charges against her.

The four bronzes – the Suthamalli Sivakami–Nataraja pair and two others – have still not been found. They are hidden somewhere in New York to this day.

But where in India are the second Nataraja and Uma from? While some people believe that they too are from the Suthamalli temple, I believe that a single notation in the Kapoor archive gives us the right answer. In a folder marked 'Sanjeevi' there are robber photos of a Nataraja and Uma. There is a note alongside, indicating that they are from a buried hoard that was probably clandestinely excavated by robbers and smuggled out of India. I believe this to be the other pair that is hidden in New York.

Think back to the great sacrifices made by our ancestors to protect our gods against looters and marauders. Think of the extent to which they went. We've already seen how, without a care for themselves, they would bury the idols to save them. We've seen how in the face of grave violence they would not open their mouths to say where their gods are hidden. We've seen how priests would pray for their sons to live, not for love or any other reason than so that someone would be alive to find and reinstate their gods after the threats had passed. For centuries upon centuries these gods have remained safe deep within the earth, until human greed and 'connoisseurs' with deep pockets and robbers make a mockery both of them and the people who sacrificed their lives to save them. The gods are auctioned off to the highest bidder and placed in glass cages. They are reduced to objects, ogled at. They remain uncared for, neither sung to nor bathed, neither fed nor loved.

All I can say is, 'Be safe, my Lords, wherever you may be, for as long as it pleases you. We will not stop looking for you and will bring you home soon.'

Author's Note

I'm sure you've heard of Harshad Mehta, Abdul Karim Telgi, Nirav Modi, Vijay Mallya, and the Satyam, 2G, Coalgate, Commonwealth Games and Adarsh scams. They are all familiar names, part of our national memory. Many of the scamsters have got away, but at least we recognize them as the thieves and crooks that they are. But if I was to mention Manu Narang,[1] Norton Simon,[2] Bumper Corporation,[3] Ben Heller,[4] LP Choraria,[5] or Vaman Narayan Ghiya,[6] would any of the names ring a bell? No, right? But these are people whose names have been associated with the biggest antiquities thefts and smuggling operations India has ever uncovered but their reputations remain unblemished in the layperson's eyes.

I did not want to let Subhash Kapoor, Sanjeevi Asokan, Deendayal, Aditya Prakash, Shantoo and Kader Batcha be added to the list – the list of anonymous thieves and smugglers who robbed us of our gods and got away with it. Together they have stolen thousands of stone and metal sculptures from our temples over the past forty years. The standing 'stock' or inventory in their godowns and warehouses runs into hundreds, and sometimes thousands, of pieces of art each. And each of these worthies has been in business for decades and decades. Can you imagine the actual scale of the loot? This, dear reader, is why I wrote this book.

But these aren't the only people involved in the plunder. There are hundreds, if not thousands, of small, petty, unknown dealers who are knowingly or unknowingly part of an illicit supply chain in Indian art. Most of them are not high profile, they don't have fancy showrooms in expensive districts of the cultural capitals of the world. Instead, many, for instance, use eBay to ply their trade in Indian antiquities. A casual Google search on Indian art throws up hundreds and thousands of stone and metal sculptures for auction and sale on websites big and small, besides those present in museums and art houses around the world. Most of the stone sculptures are cut off at the leg or are headless – these are often the signs of the force, hurry and brutality with which they are ripped out of our temples in the dead of night with crowbars and pickaxes and ropes tied to small lorries. Tempting as it may be, before you click 'Add to cart' or 'Place bid', I'd urge you to think: under what horrible circumstances were these artefacts removed from the temples to which they originally belonged? And how did they make their way outside India?

There is a long history behind this illicit trade. The looting of India's rich historical material was systematized by the British and other colonial masters. We have cases where hoards of Indian art were just picked up and shipped to the mother country – property rights and cultural ownership be damned! In some cases, art was taken from 'natives' in exchange for a bag of rice and some betel nuts – or, in one case, a pair of spectacles. Post-Independence, the diplomatic pouch was used to smuggle out sculpture and painting. Diplomats used their privileges and immunities against search and seizure to smuggle Indian art out of the country. Contemporary looting, as we have seen in this book, involves a much wider range of people, methods and technologies. Modern looters are able to smuggle even huge, seemingly immoveable, pieces out of the country and put a price tag on our invaluable heritage.

On the demand side, many auction houses, dealers, private collectors and even government-funded museums all over the world openly flout norms, rules and laws while stockpiling more and more Indian art. They practise cosmetic due diligence to tick a box, not to actually ascertain the legitimacy of an object up for sale. This is because they know that India, at least in the years gone by, did not have the will to go after the robbers who stole our patrimony.

The task of buyers and sellers is made easier by an important lubricant: the international experts who routinely authenticate clearly suspect artefacts – reputed scholars, including Padma awardees, provide advice to dealers and buyers, they value objects and write catalogues to assist in selling the loot. In fact, many scholars publish research papers based on rare artefacts, but list them as belonging to 'private collections', withholding vital information on where, who and how. It's a you-scratch-my-back-I-scratch-yours world.

And who's to stop this unholy triumvirate of robber-smugglers, buyers and experts? As far as the Indian authorities go, the less said the better. There is collusion at the highest levels – in the Idol Wing, in the customs department, in the ASI. Inspections and survey reports are rigged, investigations are deliberately goofed up, objects are valued improperly, and in several cases there is zero follow-up. In the rare instances that a few sculptures have been brought back, the recoveries were mere photo-ops, with no arrests and no efforts to follow the trail to uncover the full extent of the loot. I wrote this book, dear reader, also to show you the cosy nexuses between art dealers, museums, academia and law enforcement.

The Comptroller and Auditor General (CAG) report on the functioning of the ASI in 2013 painted a dismal picture of the custodian's slack attempts at restitution. Only nineteen artefacts were recovered between 1970 and 2000, and none between 2000 and 2012. It is fair to say that stolen Indian art is seen as fair game in the international market.

My state of Tamil Nadu has borne the brunt of looting due to the voracious American appetite for Chola bronzes. In January 2018, a response filed by the HR&CEB in the Madras High Court, stated that 1,204 sculptures (372 stone and 832 bronze) belonging to 387 temples have been stolen since 1992. It said, 'Of the more than 1200 thefts reported, only 56 had been solved and the possession of stolen items was restored only in respect of 18 cases. In cases involving theft of 385 icons/ idols from 33 temples, complaints had been closed with the items being declared as not traceable by the police department.'[7] These are only the reported thefts from sites under the protection of the HR&CE department, and do not include the vast majority of sculpture that lies in the open around the villages and towns of Tamil Nadu. If this is the situation in a fairly advanced state like Tamil Nadu, I dread to think about the robberies that take place in Madhya Pradesh, Rajasthan and Uttar Pradesh.

The rate and scale at which India's art heritage is simply vanishing should alarm you. It certainly shocks me. Conservative estimates peg the number of medium to large Indian antiquities looted at around one thousand per year. That means that on an average day, close to three important pieces are stolen and will likely disappear forever. Stop for a second and ask yourself how many priceless Natarajas like the ones stolen from Suthamalli and Sripuranthan must have disappeared forever just since the time you started reading this book.

But at a time that we should be seriously addressing this crisis – and that's what it is, a full-blown crisis – celebrated academics, politicians and law enforcers all chose to maintain that our treasures are totally safe. International lobbies throw freebies and other inducements at our 'intelligentsia' – an invitation to an international conference here, a grant there – and these eminences, in turn, have started parroting their lines. They have started pleading with the central government to dilute the provisions of our already toothless antiquities legislation to create an 'open market' for our heritage. Many want the law disallowing the export of objects older than a hundred years to be repealed.

We're told that Indian art may be better off and safer in a posh foreign museum than in a dusty old temple. Nothing could be further from the truth. Let's be clear, this is a falsehood propagated to justify crime and further the agenda of powerful international lobbies.

First, idols were not created as just pieces of art but as representations of god meant to be housed, taken care of and prayed to inside temples. They were absolutely fine for century upon century in these 'dusty old' temples until the likes of Subhash Kapoor and his apologists came on the scene. The technical brilliance and the artistry of these idols is meant to be experienced inside a temple, at the intoxicating confluence of spirituality, art and aesthetics. They are meant to inspire awe and devotion. They are meant to be seen at the same time as you hear the ringing of bells, the chanting of shlokas and mantras, the beating of drums. They are meant to be seen in the light of oil lamps or on magnificent chariots on festival days. They are meant to be seen when your senses are consumed by the smells of ghee and incense and fresh flowers and camphor. They are not meant to be seen behind cages of glass, inside sterile museums or galleries that cannot even begin to recreate the unique sensation that overtakes you when you view temple art while it is in its womb, in and around the temple's sanctum sanctorum. Our first-best option is to allow these idols to remain in their homes, in these temples.

Besides, even if you believe our gods would be better off abroad, they're not yours to sell off to the Met or to the Victoria and Albert Museum or to a private collector. They belong to village commons first and then to all of us, to the nation.

That brings me to my second point. Our founding fathers and mothers included Article 49 in our Constitution. The article states: 'It shall be the obligation of the State to protect every monument or place or object of artistic or historic interests ... of national importance, from spoliation, disfigurement, destruction, removal, disposal or export, as the case may be.' It is, therefore, incumbent on the government to protect important sites and objects. Invaluable idols cannot simply be shipped off to London and Singapore and suchlike.

The worthies who are lobbying for the weakening of our patrimony law that disallows the export of registered antiquities that are over hundred years old are full of praise for the heritage management of Greece and Italy. But guess what? Greece, Italy, and every other country with a significant material heritage have patrimony laws of their own. This is how you keep material heritage safe. So why shouldn't India keep its law in place? If our gods for some reason have to be placed inside a museum, why not an Indian one?

Things have been gradually improving – at least in the last couple of years. And we've come a long way since the scandals of the past. Take for instance something that happened in the 1970s. In 1973, an 'aggressive' stand was taken for the first time by the Government of India when it sued one of the richest men in the world, the aforementioned Norton Simon, for the Sivapuram Nataraja which he had bought for a million dollars. When asked by the *New York Times* if the piece was smuggled, Simon replied, 'Hell yes, it was smuggled. I spent between $15 and $16 million in the last two years on Asian art, and most of it was smuggled.' The Nataraja was one of the few pieces to be restituted to India. The settlement was arrived at by an out-of-court arrangement – and here's the kicker – which allowed Norton Simon to hold on to the rest of his collection of Indian art, including a fabulous Somaskanda from Sivapuram, in return for the Nataraja. Over eight hundred pieces of Indian art were laundered under cover of just this one deal! This incident highlights and typifies India's curiously ham-handed approach to cases of idol theft.

Cut to March 2018. The minister for culture tabled a report on India's success in bringing back twenty-seven artefacts between 2014 and 2018. It doesn't sound like a lot but put this figure in perspective: there were zero restitutions between 2000 and 2012. Twenty-six were due to my efforts and the efforts of the small team of committed volunteers I work with. This just shows that even a tiny team with meagre resources but with focus and devotion can make a difference. These small but important successes spur us on. We don't do this for money or awards. And we could do a lot more if we had the backing of the powers that be in our country. One hopes that this book will be read by such persons.

But more than anything else, I wrote this book to send a loud message to the crooks of the art world. There are Indians who are proud of their heritage and who will fight you tooth and nail. And we can't be swayed by your inducements. Years ago, a premium auction house offered to sponsor my 'research' and give me access to their wonderful library 'free of charge'. They also offered me a position as a consultant to pre-vet their 'Asian antiques'. I offered to do this for free, provided that they disclose the source of their antiques. And if I found a suspect antique, they had seven days to inform law enforcement of the supplier – or else I would. That was the last I heard from them. I sent their lawyer, who flew in from New York to make the offer, a thank you email, declining their gracious offer with a note at the end that said, 'Not every Indian is for sale!'

Appendix 1

Buried Hoards: Bronze Idols Buried for Safety[1]

Every now and then many bronze idols show up from under the earth. Over 200 bronzes have been found within the last ten years in Tamil Nadu alone. In most cases, the idols were deliberately buried for safety during invasion, for fear that they might be desecrated or carried away. Often the images were laid out inside a specially dug-out pit, occasionally lined with brick or stone, and filled with sand. The bronzes were carefully laid face down, securely, in the sand.

Most of the bronzes found in these treasure troves are without much damage. This shows the care with which they were concealed, with the intention of recovering them at a later date and restoring them for worship.

Scriptures on Burying Bronzes for Safety

From a careful study of the treasure trove bronzes unearthed, it is clear that such a custom had scriptural authority. Agamas do prescribe burying bronzes as a means of protection. This is what they say:

'When there is fear from robbers, enemies, invasion by the opponent kings, or disturbance in the village, in order to protect the kautuka, snapana, utsava and balibera (images used in bali offerings, festivals, bathing ceremonies, etc.) the metal images, should be hidden.

In a secret and clean place, a pit should be dug. In it sand should be spread. Over that, kusa grass should be spread. The Goddess of earth should be invoked; over this sanctified water should be sprinkled, reciting the mantra, 'apo hi stha', the acharya, the worshipping priest, the yajamana, along with the devotees should enter the shrine, offer salutation to the God, and obtain permission from the God, stating that 'Lord, so long as there is fear, till such time be you be pleased to remain living in this earth'. Then the divine power from the metal image should be transferred to the main deity. If there is no main image, it should be invoked in the heart (of the priest) uttering the mantra 'pratad visnus tapate'; the image should be carefully placed in the pit in order, reciting the mantra 'yad vaisnava'; the head (of the image) should be laid facing east. The pit should be closed either with sand or earth. The mouth of the pit should be closed tightly. Then one should enter the shrine again, adore the main image; a kurca of kusa grass should be made, the divine power should be transferred again from the main image to the kurca and the same should be worshipped. If more than one month passes, the kurca should be discarded, a new one made in its place and worshipped.

If the conditions improve, the metal image should be retrieved, cleaned with tamarind and punyaha rite should be performed.'[2]

A series of rites are then prescribed for restoring the image to worship. Similarly, different rites are prescribed for images which lay concealed for six months or over one year.

Thus, in the face of a hostile enemy, the temple custodians secured their gods by burying them in the soil for later retrieval. To this day, every year, Tamil Nadu continues to report numerous such treasure trove finds which raises a vital question. When the threat passed, why were they not recovered?

The most plausible answer, sadly, is that in all likelihood the custodians were killed or were driven away for long periods. But despite the torture and threat of death, they chose to keep the location of their gods secret. Such was their valour and supreme sacrifice, an act of ultimate defiance.

Appendix 2

Provenance and Art Loss Register

Provenance, from the French *provenir*, 'to come from', refers to the chronology of the ownership, custody or location of a historical object.

What is considered 'good provenance'?
- A signed certificate or statement of authenticity from a widely respected and recognized authority or expert on the artist.
- An exhibition or gallery sticker attached to the art.
- A statement, either verbal or written, from the artist.
- An original gallery sales receipt or receipt directly from the artist.
- A film or recording or photograph of the artist talking about the art or posed next to the art.
- An appraisal from a recognized authority or expert on the artist.
- Names of previous owners of the art.
- Letters or papers from recognized experts or authorities discussing the art.

- Newspaper or magazine articles mentioning or illustrating the art.
- A mention or illustration of the art in a book or exhibit catalogue.
- Verbal information related by someone familiar with the art or who knows the artist and who is qualified to speak authoritatively about the art.[1]

The Subhash Kapoor cases referred to in this book demonstrate the actions of a master at work. Kapoor painstakingly built up a thread of 'good provenances'. He loaned his stolen goods to museum exhibitions and even to hotels for temporary display, thereby creating fantastic histories for his objects. Often some renowned experts also provided authentication of the objects.

But the most curious of the provenances in Kapoor's arsenal are the ALR certificates he obtained. On the internet, the ALR lists its profile thus:

> Experts around the world use our services to check the provenance of items before they buy or handle them and to record items they own or that have been lost to maximize their chances of recovery.
>
> The ALR is the world's largest private database of lost and stolen art, antiques and collectables. Its range of services includes item registration, search and recovery services to collectors, the art trade, insurers and worldwide law enforcement agencies. These services are efficiently delivered by employing state of the art IT

technology and a team of specially trained professional art historians ...

Conceptually, there are two aspects to the business.

First, by encouraging ... the registration of all items of valuable possessions on the database ... the ALR acts as a significant deterrent on the theft of art. Criminals are now well aware of the risk, which they face in trying to sell on stolen pieces of art.

Second, by operating a due diligence service to sellers of art and also being the worldwide focus for any suspicion of illegitimate ownership, the ALR operates a recovery service to return works of art to their rightful owners. In recent years, the service has been extended to negotiate compensation to the victims of art theft and a legitimizing of current ownership.[2]

Let's look at the text of one certificate issued by the ALR for the Sripuranthan Nataraja.

ALR ref: AOP 260-4 dated April 20th 2007.
We have now carried out a search of the Art Loss Register's database for the following item.
Item: Shiva Nataraja
Civilization: Tamil Nadu
Date Period: 11th–12th Century, Chola Period.
Country of Origin: South India
Medium: Bronze
Dimensions: 52 inches
Provenance provided: Not Provided

We certify that this item has not, to the best of our knowledge, been registered as stolen or missing on our database of stolen and missing art nor has a claimant reported this work to us as a loss between 1933 and 1945. It should, however, be noted that:

- Not every loss or theft is reported to us
- The database does not contain information on illegally exported artefacts unless they have been reported as stolen
- The ALR does not have details of all works of art confiscated, looted or subjected to a forced seizure or forced sale between 1933 and 1945

It is also important for you to note that this certificate is no indication of authenticity of the item.

We do not guarantee the provenance of any item against which we have made a search. Your search with the Art Loss Register demonstrates due diligence but may not excuse you undertaking further research or providing further information where known. Should we become aware of any abuse of this Certificate we may find it necessary to take action.

If we can be of service to you again, please do not hesitate to contact us.

It is really baffling that such a certificate is considered part of due diligence. All it says is 'this object is not on our database of stolen objects, which is not exhaustive in the first place'. The period range of 1933 to1945 clearly points to the fact that the ALR's primary purpose is the restitution of art stolen/confiscated/immorally obtained by the Nazis.

Consider the Chola bronze under question. Photographing temple bronzes is a serious no-no in many temples that are under worship for religious reasons. Even in cases where they do permit photographs, hardly any thefts are reported. And even if they do report the theft, temples in Tamil Nadu are already so impoverished that they cannot afford to pay a hefty registration fee to a for-profit outfit in London in order to list their idols on the ALR's database of stolen art. The law enforcement agencies in India don't use the ALR's services either. Considering that Interpol has its own stolen artworks database which allows free registration of stolen works, why would someone want to even go to the ALR? Knowing all this, how can any museum or institution accept the ALR's certificate as a part of meaningful due diligence?

I'd be curious to know how many works of reported-stolen Indian art the ALR even has in its register. I'd also love to know how many certificates the ALR has given to Art of the Past. And how many to other dealers of Indian art.

My suspicion is that if the ALR released the list of artefacts for which it gave certificates to Art of the Past, as well as other dealers in Indian art, we would have a bunch of solid leads on potentially illicitly exported and stolen art. Of course, there may be many genuine cases, but we need to start from somewhere and this is as good as any.

Appendix 3

List of Museums and Institutions Associated with Art of the Past and Subhash Kapoor

The text as it appears on an archived page of the Art of the Past website (28 November 2011) is as below:

Affiliations

Art of the Past operates within an extensive business network of organizations, museums and institutions, publishers and bookstores, researchers, private collectors, and additional affiliations.

Organizations

AADNY Asia Week New York | www.asianartdealersny.com

The American Council for Southern Asian Art | www.acsaa.us

Asianart.com | www.asianart.com

Asian Art in London | www.asianartinlondon.com

The British Museum, Diploma in Asian Art | www.britishmuseum.org/.../diploma_in_asian_art.aspx

Christie's Education Master's Programs |
www.christieseducation.com/ny_mastersprogs.html
Copal Art | www.copalart.com
The Indo-American Arts Council | www.iaac.us
Osian's-Swaraj for the Arts | www.osians.com
SAIS South Asia Studies Program | www.sais-jhu.edu/
southasia
Sotheby's Institute of Art | www.sothebysinstitute.com

Museums and Institutions
Americas
Arthur M. Sackler Gallery, Freer Gallery, Smithsonian
Institution | www.asia.si.edu
The Art Institute, Chicago | www.artic.edu/aic/
Asia Society | www.asiasociety.org
Asian Art Museum of San Francisco | www.asianart.org
Baltimore Museum of Art | www.artbma.org
Brooklyn Museum of Art | www.brooklynmuseum.org
Chinese Culture Center of San Francisco | www.c-c-c.org
Cleveland Museum of Art | www.clevelandart.org
Dallas Museum of Art | www.dm-art.org
Denver Art Museum | www.denverartmuseum.org
Frick Collection | www.frick.org
J. Paul Getty Museum | www.getty.edu/museum
Harvard University Art Museums |
www.harvardartmuseums.org
High Museum of Art Atlanta | www.high.org
Honolulu Academy of Arts | www.honoluluacademy.org
Kimbell Art Museum | www.kimbellart.org

The Los Angeles County Museum of Art | www.lacma.org

Lowe Art Museum | www6.miami.edu/lowe

Metropolitan Museum of Art | www.metmuseum.org

Milwaukee Art Museum | www.mam.org

Minneapolis Institute of Arts | www.artsmia.org

The Montreal Museum of Fine Arts | www.mmfa.qc.ca/en

Museum of Fine Arts, Boston | www.mfa.org

Museum of Fine Arts, Houston | www.mfah.org

The Museum of Modern Art | www.moma.org

National Gallery of Art, Washington, DC |
www.nga.gov

National Gallery of Canada | www.gallery.ca/english

Nelson-Atkins Museum of Art | www.nelson-atkins.org

New Orleans Museum of Art | www.noma.org

Newark Museum | www.newarkmuseum.org

Peabody Essex Museum | www.pem.org

Philadelphia Museum of Art | www.philamuseum.org

Phoenix Art Museum | www.phxart.org

Royal Ontario Museum, Toronto | www.rom.on.ca

Rubin Museum of Art | www.rmanyc.org

San Diego Museum of Art | www.sdmart.org

Seattle Art Museum | www.seattleartmuseum.org

Textile Museum of Canada | www.textilemuseum.ca

The Trammell & Margaret Crow Collection of Asian
Art | www.crowcollection.com

Virginia Museum of Fine Arts | www.vmfa.state.va.us

The Walters Art Museum | thewalters.org

Weaving Art Museum and Research Institute |
www.weavingartmuseum.org

Europe

Art Gallery of Greater Victoria | aggv.ca

Ashmolean Museum of Art and Archaeology, University
of Oxford | www.ashmolean.org

The British Museum | www.britishmuseum.org

The Fitzwilliam Museum | www.fitzmuseum.cam.ac.uk

Linden-Museum Stuttgart, State Museum of Ethnology |
www.lindenmuseum.de/html/english

The Louvre | www.louvre.fr/llv/commun/home.
jsp?bmLocale=en

Musée des Arts Asiatiques-Guimet, Paris |
www.guimet.fr/-English

Museum für Indische Kunst, Asian Art Museum, Berlin |
www.smb.museum/smb/sammlungen

Museum für Kunst und Gewerbe, Hamburg |
www.mkg-hamburg.de

Museum für Lackkunst |
www.museum-fuer-lackkunst.de/index_en.htm

Plymouth City Museums and Art Gallery |
www.plymouth.gov.uk/museumpcmag.htm

Royal Museums of Art and History, Belgium |
www.kmkg-mrah.be/newfr

State Hermitage Museum | www.hermitagemuseum.org

Victoria and Albert Museum | www.vam.ac.uk

Asia

The Art Gallery of New South Wales, Sydney |
www.artgallery.nsw.gov.au

Asian Civilisations Museum, Singapore | www.acm.org.sg

Beijing Confucian Temple and Guo Zi Jian Museum |
www.kmgzj.com
Edo-Tokyo Museum |
www.edo-tokyo-museum.or.jp/english
Hara Museum of Contemporary Arts |
www.haramuseum.or.jp/generalTop.html
Hong Kong Museum of Art |
www.lcsd.gov.hk/ce/Museum/Arts/english
Hong Kong Museum of History | hk.history.museum/en
Idemitsu Museum of Art |
www.idemitsu.co.jp/museum/english
The Japan Ukiyo-e Museum | www.ukiyo-e.co.jp/jum-e
Kyoto National Museum | www.kyohaku.go.jp/eng
Miho Museum | www.miho.or.jp/english
The National Gallery of Australia, Canberra |
nga.gov.au/Home/Default.cfm
National Museum of China, Beijing |
www.chinamuseums.com/nationalm.htm
National Palace Museum, Taipei |
www.npm.gov.tw/en/home.htm
Peranakan Musuem | www.peranakanmuseum.sg
Raku Museum | www.raku-yaki.or.jp/e
Shanghai Museum | www.shanghaimuseum.net/en
Tokyo National Museum | www.tnm.go.jp/en
University Museum and Art Gallery, The University of
Hong Kong | www.hku.hk/hkumag

Publishers and Booksellers
Amazon | www.amazon.com
Art and Deal Magazine | www.artanddealmagazine.com

Arts of Asia | www.artsofasianet.com

Asian Art Newspaper | www.asianartnewspaper.com

Barnes & Noble | www.barnesandnoble.com

Borders | www.borders.com

Chapters | www.chapters.indigo.ca

The Epoch Times | www.epochtimes.com

Imperial Fine Books | www.imperialfinebooks.com

Marg Publications | www.marg-art.org

Orientations Magazine | www.orientations.com.hk

Additional Affiliations

Bonhams & Butterfields | www.bonhams.com/usa/asianart

China Guardian | www.cguardian.com/english

Dorotheum | www.dorotheum.com/en/auctions.html

Gros & Delettrez Auctioneers | www.gros-delettrez.
com/index.jsp?setLng=en

Ivey-Selkirk Auctioneers | www.iveyselkirk.com

Kogire-Kai Ltd | www.kogire-kai.co.jp/english

Koller | www.kollerauktionen.ch/en/index.asp

Lauritz | www.lauritz.com/Default.aspx?LanguageId=2

Maha Ganesha Blog | theemerald.wordpress.
com/2009/04/22/art-of-the-past

Phila China Limited | www.philachina.com

Phillips de Pury & Company | www.phillipsdepury.com

The Rasananda Project: The Art of India |
rasanandaproject.blogspot.com

Seoul Auction | www.seoulauction.com

Taj Pierre Hotel, New York City |
www.tajhotels.com/Luxury

Uppsala Auktionskammare, Sweden |
www.uppsalaauktion.se
Van Ham Fine Art Auctions | www.van-ham.com/?L=1
White Webb, LLC | www.WhiteWebb.com
Woolley & Wallis | www.woolleyandwallis.co.uk[1]

Notes

1. The Glamorous Life of Subhash Kapoor

1   http://www.metmuseum.org/art/collection/search/39328
2   http://www.sothebys.com/en/auctions/ecatalogue/2013/indian-and-south-asian-works-of-art-n08976/lot.277.lotnum.html
3   http://www.metmuseum.org/art/collection/search/64487
4   'The rogue's gallery: Subhash Kapoor and India's stolen artefacts', Arun Janardhanan, *Indian Express*, 17 July 2016. http://indianexpress.com/article/india/india-news-india/subhash-kapoor-arrested-extradited-idol-smuggling-stolen-2918744/
5   'History on Sale', Achintyarup Ray, *Times of India*, 23 July 2011. http://epaper.timesofindia.com/Repository/ml.asp?Ref=VE9JS00vMjAxMS8wNy8yMyMNBcjAwMjAw&Mode=HTML&Locale=english-skin-custom
6   'Gallery bought $11m worth of art from "smuggler" Subhash Kapoor', Michaela Boland, *The Australian*, 16 November 2013. https://www.theaustralian.com.au/arts/gallery-bought-11m-worth-of-art-from-smuggler-subhash-kapoor/story-e6frg8n6-1226761365873?sv=df21fe0c2fdce9220e59914e87d4b98c

2. The Suthamalli and Sripuranthan Heists

1   S.R. Balasubrahmanyam, *Early Chola Temples*, Sangam Books, 1960.
2   'Tamil Nadu Government works on special preventive law to curb temple thefts', S.H. Venkatramani, *India Today*, 30 April 1984.

https://www.indiatoday.in/magazine/crime/story/19840430-tamil-nadu-government-works-on-special-preventive-law-to-curb-temple-thefts-803012-1984-04-30

3   http://www.tneow.gov.in/IDOL/status_info.html
4   http://www.tneow.gov.in/IDOL/status_info.html
5   http://www.tneow.gov.in/IDOL/status_info.html

3. The Container from Mumbai

1   'The man who sold the world', Adam Matthews, *GQ*, 5 December 2013.https://www.gqindia.com/content/man-who-sold-world/
2   'ICE seizes statues allegedly linked to Subhash Kapoor, valued at $5 million', U.S. Immigration and Customs Enforcement website. 12 December 2012. https://www.ice.gov/news/releases/ice-seizes-statues-allegedly-linked-subhash-kapoor-valued-5-million
3   'The rogue's gallery: Subhash Kapoor and India's stolen artefacts', Arun Janardhanan, *Indian Express* 17 July 2016.
http://indianexpress.com/article/india/india-news-india/subhash-kapoor-arrested-extradited-idol-smuggling-stolen-2918744/
'Operation Hidden Idol: The struggle to bring back Indian antiquities', S. Vijay Kumar, *Swarajya*, 5 May 2015. https://swarajyamag.com/culture/operation-hidden-idol-the-struggle-to-bring-back-indian-antiquities
4   'DRI helps US Customs bust antiques scam', Renni Abraham, *DNA*, 23 March 2017. http://www.dnaindia.com/mumbai/report-dri-helps-us-customs-bust-antiques-scam-1086580
5   'Exposing a multidecade smuggling operation', Narayan Lakshman, *The Hindu* 11 November 2012. http://www.thehindu.com/todays-paper/tp-national/exposing-a-multidecade-smuggling-operation/article4086697.ece
6   Subhash Kapoor's confession note., 'TN cops send letter rogatory to US in case of smuggled idols', *Times of India*, 2 October 2012. https://timesofindia.indiatimes.com/city/chennai/TN-cops-send-letter-rogatory-to-US-in-case-of-smuggled-idols/articleshow/16638831.cms
'The rogue's gallery: Subhash Kapoor and India's stolen artefacts', Arun Janardhanan, *Indian Express*, 17 July 2016. http://indianexpress.

com/article/india/india-news-india/subhash-kapoor-arrested-extradited-idol-smuggling-stolen-2918744/

'The man who sold the world', Adam Matthews, *GQ*, 5 December 2013.

https://www.gqindia.com/content/man-who-sold-world/

7   https://www.ft.com/content/fcec428e-6b55-11e7-b9c7-15af748b60d0

5. The Emerald Linga Provides the Clue

1   'Idol thieves are adopting innovative ways', Gayatri Jayaraman, *India Today*, 18 June 2015.
    http://indiatoday.intoday.in/story/tamil-nadu-stolen-antique-idols-wing-prateep-v-philip/1/445384.html

2   *R. Venkataraman* v *The Director General of Police*
    https://indiankanoon.org/doc/68007570/

6. Indy Takes Charge

1   'Stolen Vishnu idol sent back to India', *The Hindu* 19 April 2006.
    http://www.thehindu.com/todays-paper/tp-international/Stolen-Vishnu-idol-sent-back-to-India/article16905840.ece

7. Revenge of a Spurned Lover

1   'Purchasing a major work of art for the collection', Joan Cummins Brooklyn Museum blog, 14 August 2007. https://www.brooklynmuseum.org/community/blogosphere/2007/08/14/purchasing-a-major-work-of-art-for-the-collection/

2   Ibid., 5 October 2007. https://www.brooklynmuseum.org/community/blogosphere/2007/10/05/purchasing-a-major-work-of-art-for-the-collection-part-vi/

3   http://eresources.nlb.gov.sg/newspapers/digitised/issue/straitstimes20100319-1#

8. Pedestal Inscription and an Anonymous Tip

1   'Asia Week 2010 in New York: Arts Of Asia Report,' Tuyet Nguyet
    and Robin Markbreiter, *Arts of Asia*, Vol. 40, issue 3, May–June 2010.

9. Arrest In Germany

1   https://indiankanoon.org/doc/14478654/?type=print
2   'The man who sold the world', Adam Matthews, *GQ*, 5 December
    2013. https://www.gqindia.com/content/man-who-sold-world/
3   Note dated 3 November 2011.

10. The Elusive Deendayal and the Hand-cut Nataraja

1   '13 idols stolen from Pazhavoor temple', *The Hindu*, 20 June 2005.
    http://www.thehindu.com/2005/06/20/stories/2005062004670700.
    htm
2   'Two idol smugglers held in Mumbai', R. Sivaraman, *The Hindu*, 30
    November 2016. http://www.thehindu.com/news/cities/chennai/
    Two-idol-smugglers-held-in-Mumbai/article16727431.ece
3   Ibid.
4   Ibid.
5   *R. Venkataraman* v *The Director General of Police*. https://indiankanoon.
    org/doc/68007570/
6   'Idol theft: DSP on the run', R. Sivaraman, *The Hindu*, 29 June 2017.
    http://www.thehindu.com/news/national/tamil-nadu/idol-theft-
    dsp-on-the-run/article19166544.ece
7   'DSP wanted in antique idols smuggling case arrested', R. Rajaram,
    The Hindu, 14 September 2017. http://www.thehindu.com/news/
    national/tamil-nadu/dsp-arrested-for-stealing-antique-idols/
    article19682036.ece
8   'First class facility for Basha rejected', *The Hindu*, 7 October 2017.
    http://www.thehindu.com/todays-paper/tp-national/tp-tamilnadu/
    court-rejects-suspended-dsps-plea/article19816065.ece
9   'The man who stole gods', Narayan Lakshman, *The Hindu*, 21 October
    2017. http://www.thehindu.com/opinion/op-ed/the-man-who-
    stole-gods/article19891536.ece

10 Undated note from Subhash Kapoor to Aaron Freedman.

11 *Subhash Chandra Kapoor* v *Inspector of Police*. 3 April 2012. https://indiankanoon.org/doc/14478654/

12 'SC refuses to quash warrant against idol dealer wanted in TN,' *Times of India* epaper, 22 June 2012. http://epaper.timesofindia.com/Repository/getFiles.asp?Style=OliveXLib:LowLevelEntityToPrint_TOINEW&Type=text/html&Locale=english-skin-custom&Path=TOICH/2012/06/22&ID=Ar00701

13 'The man who stole gods', Narayan Lakshman, *The Hindu*, 21 October 2017. http://www.thehindu.com/opinion/op-ed/the-man-who-stole-gods/article19891536.ece

11. The Ardhanarishvara and the Nataraja

1 'New images of stolen Nataraja surface', A. Srivathsan, *The Hindu*, 28 June 2013. http://www.thehindu.com/news/national/new-images-of-stolen-nataraja-surface/article4857658.ece

2 'New Evidence Of Stolen Idols at the National Gallery of Australia', chasingaphrodite.com, 4 June 2013. https://chasingaphrodite.com/2013/06/04/scoop-new-evidence-of-stolen-idols-at-the-national-gallery-of-australia/

3 'New images of stolen Nataraja surface', A. Srivathsan, *The Hindu*, 28 June 2013. http://www.thehindu.com/news/national/new-images-of-stolen-nataraja-surface/article4857658.ece

4 'Coming clean: Australia's Art Gallery of New South Wales releases Kapoor documents', Chasing Aphrodite blog, 25 June 2013. https://chasingaphrodite.com/2013/06/25/coming-clean-australias-art-gallery-of-new-south-wales-releases-kapoor-documents/

5 'Galleries need new standards for collecting precious artefacts', Michaela Boland, *The Australian*, 6 July 2013. https://www.theaustralian.com.au/news/inquirer/galleries-need-new-standards-for-collecting-precious-artefacts/news-story/18543c8aa412d56bf6efef0f9ed706f7?sv=50c1657cdf78aa0e613799868bb6efe0

6 'Temple idol from Tamil Nadu surfaces in Australia', A. Srivathsan, *The Hindu*, 21 July 2013. http://www.thehindu.com/news/national/

tamil-nadu/temple-idol-from-tamil-nadu-surfaces-in-australia/
article4935770.ece

7   'ICE HSI, Tamil Nadu Police arrest major India-based artifact
    smugglers', U.S. Immigration and Customs Enforcement website, 11
    November 2016. https://www.ice.gov/news/releases/ice-hsi-tamil-
    nadu-police-arrest-major-india-based-artifact-smugglers

8   'Brian Kennedy backed out of a transaction with Kapoor',
    Michaela Boland, *The Australian*, 5 November 2013. http://www.
    theaustralian.com.au/arts/visual-arts/brian-kennedy-backed-out-
    of-a-transaction-with-kapoor/news-story/38feecb9ad0f08167621
    d9c4fd97f363

9   https://nga.gov.au/AboutUs/press/RTF/ShivaNataraja_MR.rtf

10 'National Gallery of Australia defends practices despite admitting
    it may have been conned into buying stolen Indian art', Annie
    Maria Nicholson, *ABC News*, 6 March 2014. http://www.abc.net.
    au/news/2014-03-05/national-gallery-defends-practices-over-
    suspected-stolen-art/5300966

11 Ibid.

12 'Waiting for the Nataraja', Nirupama Subramanian, *The Hindu*, 17
    April 2014. http://www.thehindu.com/news/national/waiting-for-
    the-nataraja/article5920514.ece

13 'The Dancing Shiva', *ABC Net*, 24 March 2014. http://www.abc.net.
    au/4corners/the-dancing-shiva/5343282

14 Ibid.

15 'Home at last: Looted Shivas to be handed over in meeting of PMs',
    The Australian, 5 September 2014. https://www.theaustralian.com.au/
    arts/visual-arts/home-at-last-looted-shivas-to-be-handed-over-in-
    meeting-of-pms/news-story/e8addaa1534733388700e358b3b40e3b

16 'Stolen idols back from Australia but far from public view',
    A. Selvaraj and Julie Mariappan, *Times of India*, 12 September 2014.
    https://timesofindia.indiatimes.com/city/chennai/Stolen-idols-
    back-from-Australia-but-far-from-public-view/articleshow/
    42315974.cms

12. The Uma in Singapore

1 www.poetryinstone.in
2 Art of the Past advertisement in *Arts of Asia*. Vol. 36 No. 5, September–October 2006.
  Art of the Past Catalogue, September 2006.

13. Operation Hidden Idol

1 'Feds: Subhash Kapoor "one of the most prolific commodities smugglers in the world"', chasingaphrodite.com, 6 December 2012. https://chasingaphrodite.com/2012/12/06/feds-subhash-kapoor-one-of-the-most-prolific-commodities-smugglers-in-the-world/
2 https://chasingaphrodite.com/tag/kapoor-galleries/
3 *The People of the State of New York* v *Aaron Freedman.* https://www.scribd.com/document/189440692/NY-vs-Aaron-Freedman
4 'Assistant to accused antiquities smuggler pleads guilty to possessing looted items', Tom Mashberg, *The New York Times* blog, 4 December 2013. https://artsbeat.blogs.nytimes.com/2013/12/04/assistant-to-accused-antiquities-smuggler-pleads-guilty-to-possessing-looted-items/?_r=0)

15. The Associates

1 'The Kushan Buddhas: Nancy Wiener, Douglas Latchford and New Questions about Ancient Buddhas', chasingaphrodite.com, 1 February 2015. https://chasingaphrodite.com/2015/02/01/the-kushan-buddhas-nancy-wiener-douglas-latchford-and-new-questions-about-ancient-buddhas/
2 'Ghiya-wont-serve-life-term-idols-will-go-to-museum', *DNA Syndication*, 16 January 2014. http://dnasyndication.com/dna/TopNews/dna_english_news_and_features/Ghiya-wont-serve-life-term-idols-will-go-to-museum/DNJAI46059
3 'The idol thief: Inside one of the biggest antiquities-smuggling rings in history', Patrick Radden Keefe, *The New Yorker*, 7 May 2007. https://www.newyorker.com/magazine/2007/05/07/the-idol-thief

4   *The People of the State of New York* v *Nancy Wiener*. https://www.
    scribd.com/document/335100264/Nancy-Wiener-Complaint

5   http://www.asiaweekny.com/content/history

6   'A year after raids, Asia Week New York returns to the spotlight', Ralph
    Blumenthal and Tom Mashberg, *The New York Times*, 5 March 2017.
    https://www.nytimes.com/2017/03/05/arts/design/asia-week-new-
    york-returns-to-the-spotlight.html?mtrref=www.google.co.in&gwh
    =9B172AE0746FD0A0834A0C7FDFF323D9&gwt=pay.

7   'Stolen ancient jain and hindu statues worth $450,000 seized in US',
    Quint, 13 March 2016. https://www.thequint.com/news/world/
    stolen-ancient-jain-and-hindu-statues-worth-dollar450000-seized-
    in-us

8   'US returns 200 artifacts worth $100 million to India', *Economic
    Times*, 7 June 2016. https://economictimes.indiatimes.com/news/
    politics-and-nation/us-returns-200-artifacts-worth-100-million-
    to-india/articleshow/52634085.cms

9   *The People of the State of New York* v *Nancy Wiener* https://www.scribd.
    com/document/335100264/Nancy-Wiener-Complaint

10 Ibid.

16. The Nataraja and Uma Hidden in New York

1   'TN idol theft case: Absconding DSP Kader Batcha arrested',
    A. Selvaraj, *Times of India*, 14 September 2017. https://timesofindia.
    indiatimes.com/city/chennai/tn-idol-theft-case-absconding-dsp-
    kader-batcha-arrested-/articleshow/60509349.cms

2   http://culturalheritagelawyer.blogspot.in/2015/03/kapoor-idol-
    trafficking-conspirator.html
    'Kapoor idol trafficking conspirator sentenced', Cultural heritage
    Lawyer blog, 13 March 2015.

3   *The People of the State of New York* v *Selina Mohamed*. https://www.
    scribd.com/document/193125267/Selina-Mohamed-Complaint

4   *The People of the State of New York* v *Sushma Sareen*. https://www.
    scribd.com/doc/175894092/Sushma-Sareen-Complaint

Author's Note

1   *Ram Lal Narang Etc. Etc* v *State of Delhi* (Admn.), 10 January 1979.
    https://indiankanoon.org/doc/889775/

2   'Norton Simon bought smuggled idol', David L. Shirley, *The New York Times*, 12 May 1973.
    https://www.nytimes.com/1973/05/12/archives/norton-simon-bought-smuggled-idol-a-smuggled-idol-bought-by-simon.html

3   *Bumper Development Corp., Ltd.* v *Commissioner of Police of the Metropolis and Others.*

4   'Canada arrests two art dealers in import case', Grace Glueck, *The New York Times*, 28 December 1981. https://www.nytimes.com/1981/12/28/nyregion/canada-arrests-two-art-dealers-in-import-case.html

5   'Tamil Nadu Government works on special preventive law to curb temple thefts', S.H. Venkatramani, *India Today*, 30 April 1984.
    https://www.indiatoday.in/magazine/crime/story/19840430-tamil-nadu-government-works-on-special-preventive-law-to-curb-temple-thefts-803012-1984-04-30

6   *Vaman Narain Ghiya* v *State of Rajasthan*, 12 December 2008. https://indiankanoon.org/doc/234105/

7   'Over 1,000 temple idols stolen since 1992: Tamil Nadu admits in Madras High Court', PTI, *Indian Express*, 25 January 2018. http://www.newindianexpress.com/states/tamil-nadu/2018/ jan/25/over-1000-temple-idols-stolen-since-1992-tamil-naduadmits-in-madras-high-court-1763443.html

Appendix 1

1   'Archaeological finds in South India: Esālam Bronzes and copper-plates', R. Nagaswamy, *École française d'Extrême-Orient*, Vol. 76 (1987), pp. 1–51, 53–68. http://www.jstor.org/stable/43733559?loggedin=true&seq=1#page_scan_tab_contents

2   Ibid.

Appendix 2

2 Art provenance: What it is and how to verify it, ArtBusiness.com.
   http://www.artbusiness.com/provwarn.html
3 http://www.artloss.com/about-us

Appendix 3

1 https://web.archive.org/web/20111128165757/http://artofpast.
   com:80/affiliations/

Acknowledgements

This book is dedicated to the unknown artists and sculptors who created these divine idols, to the kings and chieftains who supported them, and to the priests and custodians who lovingly took care of the gods for hundreds of years, and to Rajaraja Chola who has been my guiding light.

There is a long list of people to whom I owe my thanks.

To writer Sri Kalki Krishnamurthy for his magnum opus *Ponniyin Selvan* that instilled in me an undying love for historical fiction.

To all my amazing fellow history enthusiasts who share my dream of restoring India's pride.

To my grandparents, Sri Kuppuswamy Iyer and Kamalambal, who shaped my early childhood with their simple, unwavering piety and devotion. I wish they could have seen this book come to life.

To my parents, Sri Sundaresan and Aruna, for their indomitable courage and unquestioning support in all my pursuits.

To my parents-in-law for taking pride in me and to this day saving cuttings of press reports on my work.

To my uncle Dr Kalyan for inspiring us with his pro bono work on Tamil computing and archive.

To my elder brother Cheenu for sharing his *Amar Chitra Katha* books with me when we were young and for egging me on to finish the manuscript!

To my school teachers, Miss Sundaram, Ms Ajitha Mathews and Ms Fransisco Rao who encouraged me to write and write more. To my boss Mr Nasir who encouraged me to do what I need to do for my country.

To my core team, Arvind Venkatraman and Shashwat, who left all their work at short notice to go on our unscheduled site documentation trips, and survived on bottles of Maaza and peanut candy!

To author Anusha Venkatesh for showing that it was no rocket science to write a book – in hindsight I would have definitely taken up launching rockets over writing non-fiction.

To all my friends in Chennai and Coimbatore – my patron Sri Shankar Vanavarayar for arranging my first lecture and never missing my talks, and artist Jeevanathan for always being there (and not yet painting my picture).

To the amazing team at the IFP, especially Dr Murugesan who put up with my numerous hours of picking their archives. Without their selfless work in maintaining the archives from the 1950s we would still be groping in the dark and lamenting our loss.

To Jason Felch and Michaela Boland who reinforced my trust in the press and the need for investigative and unbiased journalism.

To Sanjeev Sanyal for being a pillar of support and showing us how to stay focused while working from within the bureaucracy.

To Anuraag Saxena for helping us understand the intricacies of how things work in Delhi, the need for branding and setting up the India Pride Project and #BringOurGodsHome.

A big thanks to all our volunteers, friends from across nations who trusted our word, who knew they could share things in confidence and trusted that we would not sell out their information but act on it.

A special thanks to Juggernaut Books for realizing the importance of this subject and reaching out to me to write this book. My editor Parth Phiroze Mehrotra for helping me remain focused while we organized the zillion things that went into the making of this book. I would have him as co-author if I could. Thanks also to my editors Arushi Singh and Sanjiv Sarin.

A big thank you to all the celebrated academics and scholars who dubbed us as 'armchair enthusiasts' who should stay away from core history – your barbs spurred us on.

Finally a thousand apologies to Priya and Prithvi for all the hours that I spent away from you, sometimes physically and more often mentally. It is a burden I will carry for long but I hope the lasting legacy my work leaves behind will at least partially offset your sacrifice.

Lastly, thanks to Indy, without whom none of this would have happened.

When the gods decide to come home, they will choose the time and vehicle for their return. I am but one such vehicle assisting their homecoming.

Note on the Author

S. Vijay Kumar is a Singapore-based finance and shipping expert who is general manager of a leading ocean transportation company in South East Asia. Around 2007–08 he started a blog on Indian art called poetryinstone.in. Vijay's blog led him to a group of art enthusiasts and with them his pursuits have led him to track cases of art theft. Around 2010 Vijay also got involved with both Indian and US law enforcement agencies investigating cases of idol theft and smuggling. This book is based on his collaboration with these law enforcement agencies and relies heavily on documents he's seen and people he's spoken to during this association. Vijay has played a role in the arrests of idol thieves and smugglers. He has also had a major hand in matching stolen idols with pieces that have been acquired by museums, thereby ensuring their repatriation to India.

THE APP FOR INDIAN READERS

Fresh, original books tailored for mobile and for India. Starting at ₹10.

juggernaut.in

1

CRAFTED FOR MOBILE READING

Thought you would never read a book on mobile? Let us prove you wrong.

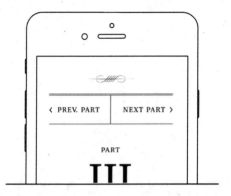

Beautiful Typography

The quality of print transferred
to your mobile. Forget ugly PDFs.

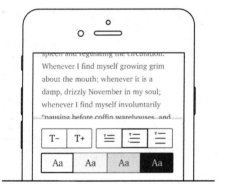

Customizable Reading

Read in the font size, spacing
and background of your liking.

AN EXTENSIVE LIBRARY

Including fresh, new, original Juggernaut books from the likes of Sunny Leone, Praveen Swami, Husain Haqqani, Umera Ahmed, Rujuta Diwekar and lots more. Plus, books from partner publishers and loads of free classics. Whichever genre you like, there's a book waiting for you.

DON'T JUST READ; INTERACT

We're changing the reading experience from passive to active.

Ask authors questions

Get all your answers from the horse's mouth.
Juggernaut authors actually reply to every
question they can.

Rate and review

Let everyone know of your favourite reads or
critique the finer points of a book – you will be
heard in a community of like-minded readers.

Gift books to friends

For a book-lover, there's no nicer gift than
a book personally picked. You can even
do it anonymously if you like.

Enjoy new book formats

Discover serials released in parts over
time, picture books including comics,
and story-bundles at discounted rates.
And coming soon, audiobooks.

LOWEST PRICES & ONE-TAP BUYING

Books start at ₹10 with regular discounts and free previews.

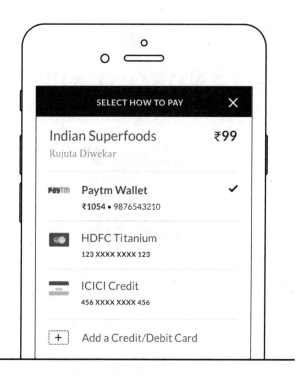

Paytm Wallet, Cards & Apple Payments

On Android, just add a Paytm Wallet once and buy any book with one tap. On iOS, pay with one tap with your iTunes-linked debit/credit card.

Click the QR Code with a QR scanner app
or type the link into the Internet browser
on your phone to download the app.

ANDROID APP

bit.ly/juggernautandroid

iOS APP

bit.ly/juggernautios

For our complete catalogue, visit www.juggernaut.in
To submit your book, send a synopsis and two
sample chapters to books@juggernaut.in
For all other queries, write to contact@juggernaut.in